OPPOSING VIEWPOINTS® SERIES

America's Global Influence

Other Books of Related Interest:

Opposing Viewpoints Series
Globalization

International Adoptions

American Values

At Issue Series
Does Outsourcing Harm America?

Is There a New Cold War?

Current Controversies Series
The U.S. Economy

The World Economy

"Congress shall make no law ... abridging the freedom of speech, or of the press."

First Amendment to the US Constitution

The basic foundation of our democracy is the First Amendment guarantee of freedom of expression. The Opposing Viewpoints series is dedicated to the concept of this basic freedom and the idea that it is more important to practice it than to enshrine it.

OPPOSING VIEWPOINTS® SERIES

America's Global Influence

Noël Merino, Book Editor

GREENHAVEN PRESS
A part of Gale, Cengage Learning

GALE
CENGAGE Learning·

Detroit • New York • San Francisco • New Haven, Conn • Waterville, Maine • London

GALE
CENGAGE Learning·

Elizabeth Des Chenes, *Managing Editor*

© 2012 Greenhaven Press, a part of Gale, Cengage Learning.

Gale and Greenhaven Press are registered trademarks used herein under license.

For more information, contact:
Greenhaven Press
27500 Drake Rd.
Farmington Hills, MI 48331-3535
Or you can visit our Internet site at gale.cengage.com

Articles in Greenhaven Press anthologies are often edited for length to meet page requirements. In addition, original titles of these works are changed to clearly present the main thesis and to explicitly indicate the author's opinion. Every effort is made to ensure that Greenhaven Press accurately reflects the original intent of the authors. Every effort has been made to trace the owners of copyrighted material.

Cover Image Alex Williamson/Ikon Images/Getty Images.

LIBRARY OF CONGRESS CATALOGING-IN-PUBLICATION DATA

America's global influence / Noël Merino, book editor.
    p. cm. -- (Opposing viewpoints)
    Includes bibliographical references and index.
    ISBN 978-0-7377-5707-1 (hardcover : alk. paper) -- ISBN 978-0-7377-5708-8 (pbk. : alk. paper)
    1. United States--Foreign relations. 2. Civilization--American influence. 3. Culture and globalization--United States. I. Merino, Noël.
    E183.7.A57 2011
    327.73--dc23
                                                        2011021027

Printed in the United States of America
1 2 3 4 5 6 7 15 14 13 12 11

Contents

Chapter 3: Are Current US Economic Policies a Good Use of America's Global Influence?

Why Consider Opposing Viewpoints?

"The only way in which a human being can make some approach to knowing the whole of a subject is by hearing what can be said about it by persons of every variety of opinion and studying all modes in which it can be looked at by every character of mind. No wise man ever acquired his wisdom in any mode but this."

John Stuart Mill

In our media-intensive culture it is not difficult to find differing opinions. Thousands of newspapers and magazines and dozens of radio and television talk shows resound with differing points of view. The difficulty lies in deciding which opinion to agree with and which "experts" seem the most credible. The more inundated we become with differing opinions and claims, the more essential it is to hone critical reading and thinking skills to evaluate these ideas. Opposing Viewpoints books address this problem directly by presenting stimulating debates that can be used to enhance and teach these skills. The varied opinions contained in each book examine many different aspects of a single issue. While examining these conveniently edited opposing views, readers can develop critical thinking skills such as the ability to compare and contrast authors' credibility, facts, argumentation styles, use of persuasive techniques, and other stylistic tools. In short, the Opposing Viewpoints Series is an ideal way to attain the higher-level thinking and reading skills so essential in a culture of diverse and contradictory opinions.

In addition to providing a tool for critical thinking, Opposing Viewpoints books challenge readers to question their own strongly held opinions and assumptions. Most people form their opinions on the basis of upbringing, peer pressure, and personal, cultural, or professional bias. By reading carefully balanced opposing views, readers must directly confront new ideas as well as the opinions of those with whom they disagree. This is not to argue simplistically that everyone who reads opposing views will—or should—change his or her opinion. Instead, the series enhances readers' understanding of their own views by encouraging confrontation with opposing ideas. Careful examination of others' views can lead to the readers' understanding of the logical inconsistencies in their own opinions, perspective on why they hold an opinion, and the consideration of the possibility that their opinion requires further evaluation.

Evaluating Other Opinions

To ensure that this type of examination occurs, Opposing Viewpoints books present all types of opinions. Prominent spokespeople on different sides of each issue as well as well-known professionals from many disciplines challenge the reader. An additional goal of the series is to provide a forum for other, less known, or even unpopular viewpoints. The opinion of an ordinary person who has had to make the decision to cut off life support from a terminally ill relative, for example, may be just as valuable and provide just as much insight as a medical ethicist's professional opinion. The editors have two additional purposes in including these less known views. One, the editors encourage readers to respect others' opinions—even when not enhanced by professional credibility. It is only by reading or listening to and objectively evaluating others' ideas that one can determine whether they are worthy of consideration. Two, the inclusion of such viewpoints encourages the important critical thinking skill of objectively evaluating an author's credentials and bias. This evaluation will illuminate an author's reasons for taking a particular stance on an issue and will aid in readers' evaluation of the author's ideas.

It is our hope that these books will give readers a deeper understanding of the issues debated and an appreciation of the complexity of even seemingly simple issues when good and honest people disagree. This awareness is particularly important in a democratic society such as ours in which people enter into public debate to determine the common good. Those with whom one disagrees should not be regarded as enemies but rather as people whose views deserve careful examination and may shed light on one's own.

Thomas Jefferson once said that "difference of opinion leads to inquiry, and inquiry to truth." Jefferson, a broadly educated man, argued that "if a nation expects to be ignorant and free . . . it expects what never was and never will be." As individuals and as a nation, it is imperative that we consider the opinions of others and examine them with skill and discernment. The Opposing Viewpoints series is intended to help readers achieve this goal.

David L. Bender and Bruno Leone,
Founders

Introduction

> *"We must use what has been called 'smart power,' the full range of tools at our disposal—diplomatic, economic, military, political, legal, and cultural—picking the right tool, or combination of tools, for each situation."*
>
> —Hillary Rodham Clinton,
> US Secretary of State

Since the end of the twentieth century, the United States arguably has been one of the most powerful countries in the world—some would say the sole global superpower. America has used its influence for decades to achieve this position in the world through a mix of hard power and soft power. The use of hard power by a country involves the use of military and economic means to influence the behavior of other countries. Military invasion, military aid, and economic sanctions are all examples of the use of hard power. By contrast, soft power involves the use of diplomacy and culture to influence the actions of other countries. Examples of soft power include humanitarian aid and cultural influence.

Joseph S. Nye Jr., professor at Harvard University's John F. Kennedy School of Government, first wrote of the concept of soft power in 1990. In a 2009 article, he explains the difference between hard and soft power:

> Power is one's ability to affect the behavior of others to get what one wants. There are three basic ways to do this: coercion, payment, and attraction. Hard power is the use of coercion and payment. Soft power is the ability to obtain preferred outcomes through attraction.

Not advocating an end to the use of all hard power, he coined the term 'smart power,' which he uses "to counter the misperception that soft power alone can produce effective foreign policy." However, he claims that in certain situations, the use of a country's soft power—its culture, values, and policies—to influence others can be more effective than hard military power: "Broader goals, such as promoting democracy, protecting human rights, and developing civil society, are not best handled with guns."[1]

America is seen as having a preference for the use of hard power, a perception that grew during the administration of President George W. Bush. Veteran of the Central Intelligence Agency and visiting professor at Georgetown University Paul R. Pillar says, "The United States exhibits an overall bias toward the instruments of hard power, and especially military power." He claims that part of the explanation for this bias is "the insufficient appreciation of the role of soft power" and "insufficient ability . . . to perceive and understand the broader side-effects of the US use of military force."[2] Critics of America's use of hard power have called for a shift in foreign policy that emphasizes soft power.

Proponents of hard power claim that soft power only works when hard power is there to back it up, and that America is uniquely equipped to use hard power effectively. Bruce Thornton, a research fellow at the Hoover Institution, claims it is naïve to believe that the soft power of diplomacy works without the threat of hard power in the background: "In the end, the threat of force has to exist somewhere in the 'world community' to punish or pressure those states that are pursuing interests counter to the interests of other states."[3]

1. Joseph S. Nye Jr., "Get Smart: Combining Hard and Soft Power," *Foreign Affairs*, July/August 2009. http://www.foreignaffairs.com/articles/65163/joseph-s-nye-jr/get-smart.
2. Paul R. Pillar, "The American Perspective on Hard and Soft Power," *National Interest*, January 4, 2011. http://nationalinterest.org/blog/paul-pillar/the-american-persective-hard-soft-power-4669.
3. Bruce Thornton, "Covenants Without Swords?" *Hoover Digest*, April 21, 2010. http://www.hoover.org/publications/hoover-digest/article/5303.

Columnist Charles Krauthammer claims that the use of America's hard power is often the only option to liberate nations around the world. He laments the decline in popularity of the use of hard power, specifically in the failure to intervene in conflicts in Zimbabwe, Burma, and Sudan, where he claims the only solution is foreign intervention. "Who's going to intervene?" he asks; "The only country that could is the country that in the past two decades led coalitions that liberated Kuwait, Bosnia, Kosovo and Afghanistan," the United States.[4]

Since the election of President Barack Obama, US foreign policy appears to be making a shift toward soft power. The national security strategy of the Obama administration warns, "our leadership around the world is too narrowly identified with military force," and notes a shift in US foreign policy: "We are strengthening alliances, forging new partnerships, and using every tool of American power to advance our objectives—including enhanced diplomatic and development capabilities with the ability both to prevent conflict and to work alongside our military."

But this shift to soft power has many critics. Abe Greenwald, an associate editor of *Commentary* magazine, claims, "The results of this emphasis on soft power have not been encouraging." He argues that the Obama administration's attempt at soft power in dealing with Iran and Russia has failed. He expresses concern that nations that oppose the United States, "will take advantage of its softness for their own malignant ends."[5] Director of the Center for Defense Studies at the American Enterprise Institute for Public Policy Research Thomas Donnelly warns, "New fashions for 'soft power' and 'smart power' can be dangerous if they are taken as a complete substitute for hard power and, particularly, military strength."[6]

---

4. Charles Krauthammer, "How Hostages, and Nations, Get Liberated," *Washington Post*, July 11, 2008. http://www.washingtonpost.com/wp-dyn/content/article/2008/07/10/AR2008071002262.html.
5. Abe Greenwald, "The Soft-Power Fallacy," *Commentary*, July 2010.
6. Thomas Donnelly, "You Cannot Outlast Us," *Daily Standard*, January 20, 2009.

In *Opposing Viewpoints: America's Global Influence,* authors present a variety of viewpoints on the subject of American power in the following chapters: What Are Some Criticisms of America's Global Influence? Is US Military Intervention Around the Globe Good for America? Are Current US Economic Policies a Good Use of America's Global Influence? and What Is the Global Impact of American Culture? The divergent viewpoints of this volume illustrate that there is wide disagreement about the extent of American influence in the world and much debate about the methods the United States uses to wield its power.

CHAPTER 1

What Are Some Criticisms of America's Global Influence?

Chapter Preface

The global financial crisis began in the United States in 2007. One of the first indicators that there was a crisis was the rise in mortgage delinquencies in the US housing market. In the decade leading up to the crisis, the US housing market experienced unprecedented growth. During that time, lending standards for mortgages became increasingly relaxed, and many people bought homes or refinanced existing mortgages with little proof of their ability to repay the loans. When borrowers began defaulting on their mortgages, it became apparent that the entire financial system was tied up in risky mortgage investments, necessitating bailouts of banks and other institutions by the US government. The housing bubble burst, many banks became insolvent, and the economy as a whole shrank, resulting in massive unemployment. Similar effects followed in Europe, and the entire globe was eventually affected in some way by the crisis.

Because of its genesis, some commentators argue that the United States was responsible for the recession. At the 2009 World Economic Forum in Davos, Switzerland, Chinese Premier Wen Jiabao blamed the financial crisis on "inappropriate macroeconomic policies" and an "unsustainable model of development characterized by prolonged low savings and high consumption," referring to the United States. Prime Minister of Russia Vladimir V. Putin expressed indignation that a year prior US delegates had said the economy was stable when, "today, investment banks, the pride of Wall Street, have virtually ceased to exist."[1] The policies of the US financial institutions and the lack of regulation have been criticized widely, both inside the United States and abroad.

1. Carter Dougherty and Katrin Bennhold, "Russia and China Blame Capitalists," *New York Times*, January 28, 2009. http://www.nytimes.com/2009/01/29/world/europe/29davos.html.

But it is not simply the US financial practices that have come under fire. Many leaders have criticized American capitalism as the ultimate cause of the crisis. French President Nicolas Sarkozy told French citizens that the crisis marked the end of laissez-faire capitalism: "A certain idea of globalization is dying with the end of a financial capitalism that had imposed its logic on the whole economy and contributed to perverting it."[2] Great Britain Prime Minister Gordon Brown said the crisis had "come from America," and Italian Prime Minister Silvio Berlusconi blamed the financial crisis on a "capitalism of adventurers" in the United States.[3]

Others deny that the United States caused the crisis and defend US capitalism. The Cato Institute's Alan Reynolds claims that a dramatic increase in the price of petroleum caused the global recession and offers proof that the United States was not the cause: "Countries with the deepest recessions have no believable connection to US housing or banking problems."[4] Another explanation, endorsed by economics professor Peter Morici, claims China is partly to blame for the financial crisis by making "it inexpensive for banks to lend us money through our homes on mortgages and second mortgages and to loan us money on credit cards and to buy cars."[5] David Boaz, executive vice president of the Cato Institute, says "the crisis can hardly be considered a failure of laissez-faire, deregulation, libertarianism, or capitalism, since it was caused

2. Steven Erlanger, "Sarkozy Stresses Global Financial Overhaul," *New York Times*, September 25, 2008. http://www.nytimes.com/2008/09/26/business/worldbusiness/26france.html.

3. Nelson D. Schwartz, "US Missteps Are Evident, but Europe Is Implicated," *New York Times*, October 12, 2008. http://www.nytimes.com/2008/10/13/business/worldbusiness/13euro.html.

. Alan Reynolds, "It Didn't Start Here: The Global Downturn Began Long Before Us," *New York Post*, April 9, 2009. http://www.nypost.com/p/news/opinion/opedcolumnists/item_gVaSb33EOiflPEOGE0BXxH/1.

5. John Ydstie, "Weighing China's Role in The Global Recession," *National Public Radio*, May 29, 2009. http://www.npr.org/templates/story/story.php?storyId=104690511.

by multiple misguided government interventions into the workings of the financial system. It was and is precisely a failure of interventionism."[6]

As the cause of the global financial crisis continues to be debated, one thing is certain: The crisis has taken its toll on America's reputation. As one of the biggest economic players in the world, the financial crisis of the early twenty-first century—even after it ends—will have a lasting effect on the global influence of the United States in economic matters.

6. David Boaz, "The Return of Big Government," *Cato Policy Report*, January/February 2009. http://www.cato.org/pubs/policy_report/v31n1/cpr31n1-1.html.

"The perception of a growing gap between the values the U.S. professes and the way it acts . . . has eroded U.S. power and influence around the world."

The George W. Bush Administration Caused a Decline in America's Reputation Worldwide

John Shattuck

In the following viewpoint, John Shattuck claims that in 2007, global opinion of the United States was at an all time low due to the George W. Bush administration's war on terror. He claims that the Bush administration weakened US power by violating human rights, ignoring international law, and disengaging from international human-rights institutions. Shattuck claims that in order to restore America's reputation, President Barack Obama must promote US foreign policy goals by working within a framework of human rights and the rule of law, in partnership with other countries. Shattuck is an international legal scholar and president of Central European University.

As you read, consider the following questions:

1. According to the author, a 2007 survey found that what percentage of the people polled in 18 countries around the world have a negative view of the United States?

2. Shattuck claims that the Bush administration's disregard for international law was made clear by a 2002 memorandum that proclaimed what?

3. According to Shattuck, what happened to important international treaties during the Bush administration?

There's a remarkable paradox in the relationship today between the United States and the rest of the world. Despite economic and military assets unparalleled in history, U.S. global influence and standing have hit rock bottom.

As an economic superpower, the U.S. has a defense budget that accounts for more than 40 percent of global military spending. But this "hard power" does not necessarily translate into real power. National-security failures abound, from the catastrophic events in Iraq to the resurgence of terrorist networks in Afghanistan and Pakistan, from the growing threat of civil war throughout the Middle East to the deepening uncertainties of the Palestinian-Israeli conflict, from the standoff with Iran to the genocide in Darfur.

The next president will have to address these crises by reestablishing America's capacity to lead. Doing so will involve working to regain international credibility and respect by reshaping American foreign policy to direct the use of power within a framework of the rule of law.

The Scale of the Problem

The United States may be strong economically and militarily, but the rest of the world sees it as ineffective and dangerous on the global stage. Less than a decade ago the situation was quite different. A 1999 survey published by the State Department Office of Research showed that large majorities in France (62 percent), Germany (78 percent), Indonesia (75 percent), Turkey (52 percent), among others, held favorable opinions of the U.S.

This positive climate of opinion fostered an outpouring of international support immediately following the September 11 attacks. The U.S. was able to assemble a broad coalition with U.N. approval to respond to the attacks and strike terrorist strongholds in Afghanistan.

Six years later global support for U.S. leadership has evaporated. In poll after poll, international opinion of the U.S. has turned sour. A January 2007 BBC survey found that 52 percent of the people polled in 18 countries around the world had a "mainly negative" view of the U.S., with only 29 percent having a "mainly positive" view. In nearly all the countries that had strong support for the U.S. in 1999 a big downward shift of opinion had occurred by the end of 2006. In France it was down to 39 percent, in Germany down to 37 percent, and in Indonesia down to 30 percent. A separate survey conducted in 2006 by the Pew Research Center revealed extremely hostile attitudes toward the U.S. throughout the Arab and Muslim world: Egypt polled 70 percent negative, Pakistan 73 percent, Jordan 85 percent, and Turkey 88 percent.

A major factor driving this negative global opinion is the way the U.S. has projected its power in the "war on terror." Four years after the Iraq invasion, U.S. military presence in the Middle East was seen by 68 percent of those polled by the BBC "to provoke more conflict than it prevents." Similarly, a poll published in April 2007 by the Chicago Council on Global Affairs showed that in 13 of 15 countries, including Argentina, France, Russia, Indonesia, India, and Australia, a majority of people agreed that "the U.S. cannot be trusted to act responsibly in the world."

The U.S. is now seen internationally to be a major violator of human rights. The BBC poll showed that 67 percent of those surveyed in 18 countries disapproved of the U.S. government's handling of detainees in Guantanamo. A survey conducted in June 2006 by coordinated polling organizations in Germany, Great Britain, Poland, and India found that majorities or pluralities in each country believed that the U.S. has tortured terrorist detainees and disregarded international treaties in its treatment of detainees, and that other governments are wrong to cooperate with the U.S. in the secret "rendition" of prisoners.

These global opinion trends have reduced the capacity of the United States to carry out its foreign policy and protect national security. The perception of a growing gap between the values the U.S. professes and the way it acts—particularly in regard to human rights and the rule of law—has eroded U.S. power and influence around the world.

In his book, *Soft Power: The Means to Success in World Politics*, Joseph Nye analyzes a nation's "ability to get what [it] wants through attraction rather than coercion." Soft power derives from "the attractiveness of a nation's culture, political ideals, and policies. When [its] policies are seen as legitimate in the eyes of others, [its] soft power is enhanced." Today, American political ideals have lost much of their global attraction because their appeal has been undermined by U.S. policies and actions that lack legitimacy in the eyes of the world. American foreign policy will continue to fail until the U.S. regains the international respect it has lost.

Fortunately, history shows that the capacity to lead can be restored when U.S. values and policies are generally in synch. During the first decade and a half of the Cold War, images of racism and segregation in the United States undercut the ability of the U.S. to project moral leadership. By the mid-1960s, however, the civil-rights movement and the leadership of Presidents Kennedy and Johnson had revived this vital capacity.

Similarly, following the disaster in Vietnam, a number of U.S. foreign-policy successes were achieved through bipartisan presidential leadership. President Ford signed the Helsinki Accords, which led to international recognition for the cause of human rights inside the Soviet bloc. President Carter mobilized democratic governments to press for the release of political prisoners held by repressive governments. President Reagan signed the Convention Against Torture and sent it to the Senate, where it was subsequently ratified. President George H.W. Bush joined with Western European governments to nurture the fledgling democracies of post-Cold War Central and Eastern Europe. President Clinton worked with NATO to end the human-rights catastrophe in Bosnia and prevent genocide in Kosovo. Each of these foreign-policy successes was achieved by linking American interests and values.

Three fundamental principles govern the exercise of soft power through the promotion of human rights and the rule of law. The first is practicing what you preach. The U.S. loses credibility when it charges others with violations it is committing itself. It reduces its ability to lead when it acts precipitously without international authority or the support of other nations. The second is obeying the law. Human rights are defined and protected by the U.S. Constitution and by conventions and treaties that have been ratified and incorporated into U.S. domestic law. The U.S. must adhere to these legal obligations if it is to project itself to other countries as a champion of human rights and the rule of law. The third is supporting international institutions. The U.S. should lead the way in reshaping existing international institutions and creating new ones, not attacking them, acting unilaterally, or turning its back whenever it disagrees with what they do.

The administration of President George W. Bush has repeatedly violated each of these principles. It has opened the U.S. to charges of hypocrisy by criticizing other governments for acting outside the rule of law and committing human-rights abuses it has committed itself. The annual *Country Reports on Human Rights Practices* issued by the State Department covers official actions such as "torture and other cruel, inhuman or degrading treatment or punishment," "detention without charge," "denial of fair public trial," and "arbitrary interference with privacy, family, home, or correspondence." These are the very practices in which the Bush administration itself has systematically engaged, compelling readers of the State Department *Country Reports* to conclude that the U.S. does not practice what it preaches. The 2006 report on Egypt, for example, criticizes the fact that Egyptian police and security forces "detained hundreds of individuals without charge," that "abuse of prisoners and detainees by police, security personnel and prison guards remained common," and that "the [Egyptian] Emergency Law empowers the government to place wiretaps . . . without warrants." These same criticisms apply to the United States.

The Bush administration has diminished a second source of soft power by flaunting basic requirements of international and domestic law. These include the Geneva Conventions, the Convention Against Torture, and the International Convent on Civil and Political Rights, and the Foreign Intelligence Surveillance Act. The result has been the creation of "law-free zones" in which foreign detainees in U.S. custody overseas have been brutally abused, thousands of foreign citizens have been held indefinitely as "unlawful combatants" without being accorded the status of prisoners of war, and repressive regimes around the world have implicitly been given the green light to crack down on political dissidents and religious and ethnic minorities in the name of fighting terrorism.

The administration's history of disregard for the established framework of international law was made clear by a 2002 memorandum, prepared by the then-White House counsel, Alberto Gonzales, proclaiming that "terrorism renders obsolete the Geneva Conventions' strict limitations on the questioning of prisoners." No recent president had questioned the basic rules of international humanitarian law in times of war. The administrations of Lyndon B. Johnson, Richard Nixon, and Gerald Ford during the Vietnam War, and George H.W. Bush during the Gulf War, all adhered to the Geneva requirements. The reasons were spelled out in a 2002 memorandum by then-Secretary of State Colin Powell, challenging the Gonzales memo. Powell warned that the White House interpretation of the Geneva Conventions would "reverse over a century of U.S. policy and practice, undermine the protections of the law of war for our troops, and [provoke] negative international reaction, with immediate adverse consequences for our conduct of foreign policy."

A third source of soft power has been undermined by the Bush administration's attacks on and disengagement from international human-rights institutions. The U.S. has been a world leader in building these institutions since the time when Eleanor Roosevelt chaired the international committee that drafted the Universal Declaration of Human Rights. The current administration has renounced that leadership by refusing to run for a seat on the new U.N. Human Rights Council and by undermining efforts to shape the new International Criminal Court (ICC). Both institutions are flawed, but as a result of the administration's disengagement the U.S. now has no influence over their future development.

Undercutting National Security

The Bush administration's record on human rights and the rule of law has undercut the capacity of the U.S. to achieve important foreign-policy goals. The erosion of America's soft power has made it more difficult for the U.S. to succeed in preventing or containing threats of terrorism, genocide, and nuclear proliferation. The denigration of American values has made the U.S. ineffective in promoting human rights and democracy. Indeed, the current administration's frequent disregard of the rule of law has jeopardized five frequently stated foreign-policy objectives.

The first is countering the threats posed by Iraq, Iran, and Afghanistan. For more than a decade these countries have topped the United States' list of dangers to international security. Strategies to reduce the violence and terrorism in Iraq and Afghanistan and to prevent Iran from exporting terrorism and acquiring nuclear weapons require a mixture of hard and soft power. But reports of CIA and U.S. military torture and mistreatment of prisoners at Abu Ghraib and other secret prisons in the region may have weakened the ability of the U.S. to counter the deterioration of human-rights conditions in Iraq and Afghanistan. Similarly, State Department criticism of the Iranian regime's political repression has been blunted by the U.S. record of detainee abuse and illegal electronic surveillance. Years after the U.S. military interventions, Iraq and Afghanistan remain major exporters of terrorism and centers of human-rights abuse. Iran is a major terrorist exporter and a human-rights disaster.

A second major stated objective of U.S. foreign policy is preventing genocide. The lesson of Rwanda was that the cost of failing to stop genocide is not only a massive killing of innocent civilians but also an ongoing humanitarian catastrophe and long-term regional instability. Following the Rwanda genocide, a doctrine of humanitarian intervention was developed under U.S. leadership and invoked, with broad international support and authority under the Genocide Convention, to end the genocide in Bosnia in 1995, and then to prevent a genocide in Kosovo in 1999. Today, that doctrine is in shambles, undermined and discredited by the Bush administration's intervention in Iraq. As a result, the U.S. has been unable to mobilize support to stop the ongoing genocide in Darfur and an entire region of Africa has been destabilized.

Addressing the challenges posed by geopolitical rivals such as China, Russia, and Cuba is a third long-standing concern of U.S. foreign policy. The Bush record has made already-complicated interactions with these countries even more difficult. China is leading the way in effectively exploiting the growing global perception that the U.S. is a human-rights violator. For several years the Chinese government has produced and publicized its own report on U.S. human-rights failings in an attempt to counter U.S. criticism of China's record. China's March 2007 report was particularly blunt: "We urge the U.S. government to acknowledge its own human rights problems and stop interfering in other countries' internal affairs under the pretext of human rights." Russian President Vladimir Putin has been similarly direct in rejecting recent U.S. criticism of the Russian government's press censorship, and Cuba has been quick to point to the U.S. record of detainee abuse at Guantanamo whenever Cuban human-rights practices are challenged by the U.S. The Bush administration has provided China, Russia, and Cuba with a convenient excuse for cracking down on dissidents and minorities under the guise of fighting terrorism within their borders.

Creating and managing strategic alliances is a fourth major U.S. foreign-policy objective. The Bush administration's record on human rights and the rule of law has alienated traditional democratic allies and complicated relations with authoritarian countries. The Council of Europe, a parliamentary assembly of elected representatives from across the continent, has condemned European governments for cooperating with the U.S. in running secret detention centers, and has called for Europe to distance itself from the Bush administration's tactics in the "war on terror." Negative European opinion about U.S. human-rights practices has made it politically difficult for European leaders to support U.S. positions on other issues. And by condoning torture, prisoner abuse, secret detention, illegal surveillance, and other violations of human rights, the administration has also undercut its ability to promote reform with authoritarian allies like Egypt, Saudi Arabia, Morocco, and Uzbekistan.

Finally, holding accountable those who commit human-rights crimes has been a bedrock objective of U.S. foreign policy since the Nuremberg trials following World War II. The U.S. has long been at the forefront of efforts to create a system of international justice, most recently in the establishment of the International Criminal Tribunals for the Former Yugoslavia and Rwanda. By opposing the International Criminal Court, the Bush administration has relinquished its leadership on these issues. The indispensability of international justice to U.S. foreign policy is illustrated by the administration's retreat in 2006 from outright opposition to the ICC to reluctant acceptance of the U.N. Security Council's referral of the Darfur genocide case to ICC jurisdiction. But this begrudging exception unfortunately proves the rule.

Repairing the Damage

The next president must make repairing the damage to American values and moral authority a top priority. Acting within a framework of the rule of law and respect for human rights will be essential to restoring America's international leadership.

The U.S. must strengthen its alliances by demonstrating it adheres to international norms in pursuing its national-security objectives. The next president should immediately announce that the U.S. will close the detention center at Guantanamo and transfer detainees to the U.S. or detainees' home countries. In addition, the president should announce that the U.S. is bound by the Geneva Conventions as a matter of law and policy. Restoring the U.S. policy of providing individualized status hearings to detainees would demonstrate respect for international norms without restricting the government's capacity to conduct lawful interrogations to obtain intelligence information about terrorist activities. Fully applying the Geneva Conventions also would not preclude the U.S. from trying detainees in military commissions.

A second means of underscoring U.S. commitment to address national-security threats within the rule of law would be to provide assistance to other countries for counterterrorism operations that comply with basic human-rights standards. "Fighting terror" has become a convenient excuse for repressive regimes to engage in further repression, often inspiring further terrorism in an increasing cycle of violence. To break this cycle, the U.S. should provide assistance and training to foreign military and law enforcement personnel in methods of fighting terrorism within the rule of law.

The U.S. should take the lead in drafting a comprehensive treaty defining and condemning terrorism within a framework of human rights. Working toward a consensus on this global issue would help counter the claim that differences in cultural values, religious beliefs, political philosophies, or justifiable ends make it impossible to define the crime of terrorism.

The president should make clear that the U.S. is prepared once again to be an active participant in strengthening the system of international law it helped create over the last half century. Important treaties have lingered for years in the Senate and should now be ratified or renegotiated. Some were signed by Republican presidents and once enjoyed bipartisan support, but have been blocked for the last seven years by the current administration and its Senate supporters. The U.S. should also rejoin negotiations on such critical issues as human rights, international justice, climate change, and nonproliferation of weapons of mass destruction. By doing so, the next president would demonstrate that globalization can be made to work within the rule of law.

The U.S. should support those seeking to promote the rule of law, democracy, and human rights in their own countries. Democracy and human-rights activists are the shock troops in the struggle against terrorism, genocide, and nuclear proliferation. But democracy can never be delivered through the barrel of a gun. Assistance to those who are working to build their own democratic societies must be carefully planned and targeted, sustained over time, and based on a thorough understanding of the unique circumstances and profound differences among cultures, religions, and countries. A new U.S. government must work within an international framework, not unilaterally and preemptively, to assist those struggling around the world to bring human rights to their own societies.

Finally, the U.S. should join with other countries, alliances, and international organizations to reassert America's role in working to prevent or stop genocide and crimes against humanity. The president should invoke the doctrine of humanitarian intervention that was applied in Bosnia and Kosovo in the 1990s to address the genocide in Darfur. Extensive diplomatic and economic tools can be used to head off an impending genocide, but international military intervention remains available under international law if all other avenues have been exhausted.

By recommitting the U.S. to a foreign policy conducted within a framework of human rights and the rule of law, the next president can restore America's moral leadership in the world—and by so doing, enhance American power and security.

"Opinions of the U.S., which improved markedly in 2009 in response to Obama's new presidency, also have remained far more positive than they were for much of George W. Bush's tenure."

The Barack Obama Administration Has Improved America's Reputation Worldwide

Pew Research Center

In the following viewpoint, the Pew Research Center reports that, based on its 2010 survey, global opinion of the United States is better than it was during the presidency of George W. Bush. The Center claims that ratings of the United States are favorable in most parts of the world except for in Muslim countries and Mexico. Global opinion about President Barack Obama, the Center says, is higher than global opinion of President George W. Bush. However, the Center asserts that US foreign policy still has

"Obama More Popular Abroad Than at Home: Global Image of U.S. Continues to Benefit," June 17, 2010, pp. 1–5, the Pew Global Attitudes Project, a project of the Pew Research Center. Reproduced by permission.

many critics around the globe. The Pew Research Center is a nonpartisan organization that provides information on the issues, attitudes, and trends shaping America and the world.

As you read, consider the following questions:

1. According the Pew Research Center, what percentage of people in France and Germany said they have a favorable view of the United States?

2. The author reports that in non-Muslim nations, the median overall approval of President Barack Obama's policies is at what percentage rating?

3. How many nations out of twenty-two surveyed approve of President Obama's handling of the Israeli-Palestinian conflict?

As the global economy begins to rebound from the great recession, people around the world remain deeply concerned with the way things are going in their countries. Less than a third of the publics in most nations say they are satisfied with national conditions, as overwhelming numbers say their economies are in bad shape. And just about everywhere, governments are faulted for the way they are dealing with the economy.

Yet in most countries, especially in wealthier nations, President Barack Obama gets an enthusiastic thumbs up for the way he has handled the world economic crisis. The notable exception is the United States itself, where as many disapprove of their president's approach to the global recession as approve.

This pattern is indicative of the broader picture of global opinion in 2010. President Barack Obama remains popular in most parts of the world, although his job approval rating in the U.S. has declined sharply since he first took office. In turn, opinions of the U.S., which improved markedly in 2009 in response to Obama's new presidency, also have remained far more positive than they were for much of George W. Bush's tenure.

Ratings of America are overwhelmingly favorable in Western Europe. For example, 73% in France and 63% in Germany say they have a favorable view of the U.S. Moreover, ratings of America have improved sharply in Russia (57%), up 13 percentage points since 2009, in China (58%), up 11 points, and in Japan (66%), up 7 points. Opinions are also highly positive in other nations around the world including South Korea (79%), Poland (74%), and Brazil (62%).

The U.S. continues to receive positive marks in India, where 66% express a favorable opinion, although this is down from last year when 76% held this view. America's overall image has also slipped slightly in Indonesia, although 59% still give the U.S. a positive rating in the world's largest predominantly Muslim nation.

Publics of other largely Muslim countries continue to hold overwhelmingly negative views of the U.S. In both Turkey and Pakistan—where ratings for the U.S. have been consistently low in recent years—only 17% hold a positive opinion. Indeed, the new poll finds opinion of the U.S. slipping in some Muslim countries where opinion had edged up in 2009. In Egypt, America's favorability rating dropped from 27% to 17%—the lowest percentage observed in any of the Pew Global Attitudes surveys conducted in that country since 2006.

Closer to home, a special follow-up poll found America's favorable rating tumbling in Mexico in response to Arizona's enactment of a law aimed at dealing with illegal immigration by giving police increased powers to stop and detain people who are suspected of being in the country illegally. Only 44% of Mexicans gave the U.S. a favorable rating following the signing of the bill, compared with 62% who did so before the bill passed.

The new survey by the Pew Research Center's Global Attitudes Project, conducted April 7 to May 8, also finds that overall opinion of Barack Obama remains broadly positive in most non-Muslim nations. In these countries, the national median confidence in Obama to do the right thing in world affairs is 71%, and overall approval of his policies is 64%. In particular, huge percentages in Germany (88%), France (84%), Spain (76%) and Britain (64%) say they back the president's policies. Similarly in the two African nations polled Obama gets high marks—89% of Kenyans and 74% of Nigerians approve of his international policies.

Muslims Grow Disillusioned About Obama

Among Muslim publics—except in Indonesia where Obama lived for several years as a child—the modest levels of confidence and approval observed in 2009 have slipped markedly. In Egypt the percentage of Muslims expressing confidence in Obama fell from 41% to 31% and in Turkey from 33% to 23%. Last year only 13% of Pakistani Muslims expressed confidence in Obama, but this year even fewer (8%) hold this view. And while views of Obama are still more positive than were attitudes toward President Bush among most Muslim publics, significant percentages continue to worry that the U.S. could become a military threat to their country.

Obamamania Tempers

In countries outside of the Muslim world, where the president's ratings remain generally positive, his standing is not quite as high in 2010 as it was a year ago. The new poll found fewer in many Asian and Latin American countries saying they have confidence in Obama and approve of his policies generally, and even in Europe the large majorities responding positively to his foreign policy are not quite as large as they were in 2009.

Besides declines in overall confidence in some countries, *strong* endorsement of Obama eroded in countries where he

A Rise in Confidence in the United States

Will Do Right Thing in World Affairs

% Confident	Bush 2008 %	Obama 2010 %
U.S.	37	65
France	13	87
Germany	14	90
Spain	8	69
Britain	16	84
Poland	41	60
Russia	22	41
Turkey	2	23
Egypt	11	33
Jordan	7	26
Lebanon	33	43
China	30	52
Japan	25	76
S. Korea	30	75
Pakistan	7	8
India	55	73
Indonesia	23	67
Argentina	7	49
Mexico	16	43
Nigeria	55	84
Kenya	72	95

Pew Research Center,
"Obama More Popular Abroad Than at Home:
Global Image of U.S. Continues To Benefit," June 17, 2010, p. 2.

remains broadly popular. Notably, in Britain, France, Germany, and Japan, fewer this year say they have *a lot* of confidence in Obama's judgment regarding world affairs, while more say *some* confidence; still there was no increase in the percentage expressing *no* confidence in Obama in these countries.

Even though Obama has called the Arizona immigration law "misdirected," it is nonetheless having a negative impact on views of him in Mexico. Prior to the law's passage, 47% of Mexicans had confidence in Obama's international leadership, but after passage only 36% held this view. More specifically, 54% of Mexicans say they disapprove of the way Barack Obama is dealing with the new law, and as many as 75% say that about Arizona Gov. Jan Brewer.

Disagreeing While Not Disapproving

Perhaps more significant than Obama's small declines in ratings is that a generally positive view of him and the U.S. coexists with significant concerns about the American approach to world affairs and some key policies. This was not the case in the global surveys taken during President Bush's terms in office, when specific criticism ran hand in hand with anti-American and anti-Bush sentiment.

Then, as now, one of the most frequent criticisms of U.S. foreign policy is that in its formulation it does not take into account the interests of other countries. This is the prevailing point of view in 15 of 21 countries outside of the U.S. Somewhat fewer people in most countries level this charge than did so during the Bush era. Currently, the median number saying that the U.S. acts unilaterally is 63%; in 2007 a median of 67% expressed that view.

In contrast to the Bush years, there is substantial majority support for U.S. anti-terrorism efforts in Britain, France, Spain and Germany. The new poll also found major increases in support of the American efforts in two countries that have been struggling with terrorism of late: Indonesia and Russia, where roughly seven-in-ten say they back the U.S. in this regard. Publics in India, Brazil, Kenya and Nigeria also express strong support for U.S.-led efforts to combat terrorism. However, opposition to these policies is particularly strong in most Muslim countries, and it is also substantial in many nations where the U.S. is fairly well-regarded, including Japan and South Korea.

The war in Afghanistan remains largely unpopular. In Germany, which has the third largest contingent of allied troops in Afghanistan, nearly six-in-ten people favor withdrawal from that country. Opinions are more divided in NATO allies Britain, France and Poland. In most other countries surveyed, majorities or pluralities also oppose the NATO effort.

Global opinion of Barack Obama's dealing with world trouble spots parallels general opinion of U.S. policies in these areas. With regard to Afghanistan, Iraq and Iran, the polling found as many countries approving as disapproving of his handling of these issues. However, the American president gets his worst ratings for dealing with another world problem for which the U.S. is often criticized: the Israeli-Palestinian conflict. Of 22 nations surveyed including the U.S., in only three nations do majorities approve of Obama's handling of the dispute: France, Nigeria and Kenya.

In sharp contrast to criticisms and mixed reviews of Obama's handling of geo-political problems, Obama not only gets good grades for the way he has handled the world economic crisis, but also for dealing with climate change. In most countries, people approve of Obama's climate change efforts. France is a notable exception, with a 52%-majority disapproving, despite the country's approval of his other policies.

> *"The central question before us is whether to abandon our traditional sense of ourselves as an exceptional nation."*

Belief in American Exceptionalism Should Be Conserved and Celebrated

Richard Lowry and Ramesh Ponnuru

In the following viewpoint, Richard Lowry and Ramesh Ponnuru contend that American exceptionalism is under attack and needs to be conserved. Lowry and Ponnuru claim that America's belief in liberty, individualism, populism, laissez-faire economics, religion, and military defense form the core of American exceptionalism that has existed since the nation's founding. The authors worry that President Barack Obama's policies will undermine American exceptionalism, and they claim that the objection to Obama's policies is a sign that Americans are reluctant to abandon the doctrine. Lowry is the editor and Ponnuru is a senior editor of National Review, *a conservative American news magazine.*

Richard Lowry and Ramesh Ponnuru, "An Exceptional Debate: The Obama Administration's Assault on American Identity," *National Review* online, vol. 62, March 8, 2010. Copyright © 2010 National Review Online. All rights reserved. Reproduced by permission.

As you read, consider the following questions:

1. According to the authors, what percentage of Americans expect to get rich?

2. According to Lowry and Ponnuru, what percentage of Americans believe in God?

3. The authors claim that since the 1940s, America has held what role in the world?

What do we, as American conservatives, want to *conserve*? The answer is simple: the pillars of American exceptionalism. Our country has always been exceptional. It is freer, more individualistic, more democratic, and more open and dynamic than any other nation on earth. These qualities are the bequest of our Founding and of our cultural heritage. They have always marked America as special, with a unique role and mission in the world: as a model of ordered liberty and self-government and as an exemplar of freedom and a vindicator of it, through persuasion when possible and force of arms when absolutely necessary. . . .

The Core of American Exceptionalism

To find the roots of American exceptionalism, you have to start at the beginning—or even before the beginning. They go back to our mother country. Historian Alan Macfarlane argues that England never had a peasantry in the way that other European countries did, or as extensive an established church, or as powerful a monarchy. English society thus had a more individualistic cast than the rest of Europe, which was centralized, hierarchical, and feudal by comparison.

It was, to simplify, the most individualistic elements of English society—basically, dissenting low-church Protestants—who came to the eastern seaboard of North America. And the most liberal fringe of English political thought, the anti-court "country" Whigs and republican theorists such as James Harrington, came to predominate here. All of this made America an outlier compared with England, which was an outlier compared with Europe. The U.S. was the spawn of English liberalism, fated to carry it out to its logical conclusion and become the most liberal polity ever known to man. . . .

Exact renderings of the creed differ, but the basic outlines are clear enough. The late Seymour Martin Lipset defined it as liberty, equality (of opportunity and respect), individualism, populism, and laissez-faire economics. The creed combines with other aspects of the American character—especially our religiousness and our willingness to defend ourselves by force—to form the core of American exceptionalism.

The Greatest Economic Power

Liberty is the most important element of the creed. To secure it, the Founders set about strictly limiting government within carefully specified bounds. Immediately upon the collapse of British government in America, the states drew up written constitutions and neutered their executives. They went as far as they could possibly go to tame the government—indeed, they went farther, and had to start over to get a functioning state. But even this second try produced a Constitution that concentrated as much on what government could not do as on what it could. . . .

In the latitude provided by this relatively light-handed government, a commerce-loving, striving, and endlessly inventive people hustled its way to become the greatest economic power the world has ever known.

In America, there really hasn't been a disaffected proletariat—because the proletariat has gotten rich. [German philosopher] Friedrich Engels had it right when he carped that "America is so purely bourgeois, so entirely without a feudal past and therefore proud of its purely bourgeois organization."

The traditional Marxist claim about the U.S. was that it was governed by the executive committee of the bourgeoisie. This was not intended as a compliment, but it was largely true. Look at the archetypal American, Benjamin Franklin, whose name comes from the Middle English meaning freeman, someone who owns some property. [French Emperor] Napoleon [Bonaparte] dismissed the British as "a nation of shopkeepers"; we are a nation of Franklins.

Abraham Lincoln, a de facto Founding Father, is an exemplar of this aspect of America. "I hold the value of life," Lincoln said, "is to improve one's condition." There are few things he hated more than economic stasis. He couldn't abide Thomas Jefferson's vision of a nation of yeoman farmers living on their land forevermore, blissfully untouched by the forces of modern economic life. (Appropriately enough, Jefferson died broke.) Lincoln captured the genius of American life when he said, "The man who labored for another last year, this year labors for himself, and next year he will hire others to labor for him."

American Attitudes Toward Wealth

That sentiment is at the heart of the American economic gospel. American attitudes toward wealth and its creation stand out within the developed world. Our income gap is greater than that in European countries, but not because our poor are worse off. In fact, they are better off than, say, the bottom 10 percent of Britons. It's just that our rich are phenomenally wealthy.

This is a source of political tension, but not as much as foreign observers might expect, thanks partly to a typically American attitude. A 2003 Gallup survey found that 31 percent of Americans expect to get rich, including 51 percent of young people and more than 20 percent of Americans making less than $30,000 a year. This isn't just cockeyed optimism.

America remains a fluid society, with more than half of people in the bottom quintile pulling themselves out of it within a decade.

And so we arrived in the 21st century still a country apart. Prior to its recent run-up, total government spending was still only about 36 percent of GDP [gross domestic product] in the U.S. In Europe, the figure was much higher—44 percent in Britain, 53 percent in France, and 56 percent in Sweden. (The difference is starker when only non-defense spending is compared.)

A Democratic Country

Politically, we have always been more democratic, more populist than other countries. [Irish philosopher] Edmund Burke said of the low-church Protestants who flocked here, "They represent the dissidents of dissent and the protest wing of the Protestant religion." The Scotch-Irish who settled the hinterlands were even more cussed. It wasn't very easy to tell any of these people what to do, as colonial governors learned to their regret.

Later, in the 19th century, the Federalists tried to create a kind of aristocracy. They got rich and set themselves up as grandees. Knowing that many members of this self-designated ruling class started life in the same state they had, their neighbors didn't take kindly to these pretensions. The Federalist party wasn't long for this world—a lesson in how poorly elite condescension plays in America.

Today, we still have more elections for more offices more often than other countries. Even many judges and law-enforcement officials are elected. In the federal government, political appointees have greater sway over the civil service than is the case in other developed countries. As Edward C. Banfield and James Q. Wilson have written, "There is virtually no sphere of 'administration' apart from politics."

In Europe, the opposite is the case and has become more so with the rise of the European Union [EU]. Brussels is arrogating more decision-making to itself, removed from the locus of democratic accountability in individual nations. When important EU questions are put to the voters in referenda, there is only one correct answer, and when nations vote the "wrong" way, elections are held over and over again until they succumb. This European-style politics of bureaucratic, elite high-handedness is dangerous in its undemocratic nature and anathema to the American character.

A Youthful, Religious Country

We have managed to preserve a remarkable national spirit. At over 70 percent, more Americans express pride in their country than Western Europeans do in theirs. In terms of demography, we are the youngest advanced country in the world, and our population continues to grow as that of Western Europe is projected to decline.

Americans are more religious than Europeans. In the 18th century, American religious dissenters supported overthrowing state-supported churches because it would allow them to compete on an even playing field with other denominations. In that competition, America saw an explosion of religious feeling and became the most evangelical country in the world.

Religion gained authority and vitality from its separation from the state, and religion-inspired reform movements, from abolitionism to the civil-rights movement, have been a source of self-criticism and renewal. Today, 73 percent of Americans believe in God, compared with 27 percent of Frenchmen and 35 percent of Britons, according to a 2006 *Financial Times* survey.

All of this means that America has the spirit of a youthful, hopeful, developing country, matched with the economic muscle of the world's most advanced society and the stability of its oldest democratic institutions.

Obama on Exceptionalism

A good way to discern what motivates [President Barack] Obama is to ask a simple question: What is his dream? Is it the American dream? Is it Martin Luther King's dream? Or something else? It is certainly not the American dream as conceived by the founders. They believed the nation was a "new order for the ages." A half-century later Alexis de Tocqueville wrote of America as creating "a distinct species of mankind." This is known as American exceptionalism. But when asked at a 2009 press conference whether he believed in this ideal, Obama said no. America, he suggested, is no more unique or exceptional than Britain or Greece or any other country.

Dinesh D'Souza,
"Obama's Problem with Business"
Forbes Asia Magazine, *September 27, 2010.*

The Exportation of American Liberty

This national spirit is reflected in our ambitious and vigorous foreign policy. We were basically still clinging to port cities on the eastern seaboard when we began thinking about settling the rest of the continent. There never was a time when we were an idyllically isolationist country. We wanted to make the continent ours partly as a matter of geopolitics: France, Spain, and Britain were wolves at the door. But throughout our history, we have sought not just to secure our interests abroad, but to export our model of liberty.

This missionary impulse is another product of the American Revolution, which took English liberties and universalized them. The Founders thought we would play an outsized role in the world from the very beginning. We would be an "empire of liberty," Jefferson said. He believed that the flame of liberty, once lit on our shores, would inevitably consume the world.

This strain in American thought was expressed throughout the 20th century in the democratic idealism of [Presidents Woodrow] Wilson, [Franklin Delano Roosevelt] FDR, and [Jimmy] Carter. At its best, this tendency has been tempered by prudence and realism so as to avoid foolish adventurism. [President Ronald] Reagan exemplified the appropriate mix, as he avoided (with the painful exception of Lebanon) risky foreign interventions at the same time he ushered the Soviet Union to its grave through a shrewd combination of hard and soft power.

But make no mistake: America is still a martial nation with a no-nonsense, hit-back-harder Jacksonian temperament when challenged. Historically, it has responded to attacks, whether at Fort Sumter or Pearl Harbor, with overwhelming force and the maximum plausible effort to spread our democratic system. In this sense, George W. Bush's response to 9/11 [2001, terrorist attacks]—two foreign wars, both justified partly as exercises in democratization—was typically American.

Our defense spending constituted half of the world's defense spending in 2003. With a few exceptions (the British, the Canadians), we are the only Western nation that is able and willing to conduct major combat operations overseas. Even when Afghanistan was considered "the good war" by the rest of the world, we had to do most of the heavy lifting.

None of this is to say, of course, that America is perfect. No nation can be. But one can only regard with wonderment what America stands for and all that it has accomplished in its amazing, utterly distinct adventure in liberty. . . .

Obama's Anti-Idealism

President [Barack] Obama's first year in office should be seen in the context of contemporary liberalism's discomfort with American exceptionalism.

The president has signaled again and again his unease with traditional American patriotism. As a senator he notoriously made a virtue of not wearing a flag pin. As president he has been unusually detached from American history: When a foreign critic brought up the Bay of Pigs, rather than defend the country's honor he noted that he was a toddler at the time. And while acknowledging that America has been a force for good, he has all but denied the idea that America is an exceptional nation. Asked whether he believed in American exceptionalism during a European trip last spring, Obama said, "I believe in American exceptionalism, just as I suspect that the Brits believe in British exceptionalism and the Greeks believe in Greek exceptionalism." (Is it just a coincidence that he reached for examples of former hegemons?) . . .

Since the 1940s America has been the crucial undergirding of the international order. Its power and sway are a stabilizing influence in every region of the world, and it provides international public goods, from the policing of sea lanes to humanitarian interventions. It is also, in keeping with its missionary history, the chief exponent of liberty in the world.

Obama is turning his back both on the overarching vision of freedom and on the prudence, and mislabeling his approach "realism." He has been positively allergic to the word "democracy." His administration has shown very little interest in defending human rights around the world, whether in China or in Cuba. During the Iranian election crisis, he was even cooler to the protesters in the streets than the Europeans were.

His hesitance to advocate American ideals is not a return to the realpolitik of [President Richard] Nixon or the first [President George H.W.] Bush. A deep naïveté informs his policy. He believes that our enemies can be persuaded, merely through sweet talk and blandishments, to abandon their cold-blooded interests and their most deeply held ambitions. This is impossible without developing the kind of leverage over them in which Obama seems to have little interest. Yes, Reagan negotiated with the Soviets, but only when they had a leader who was a reformer and the arms build-up and the prospect of SDI [Strategic Defense Initiative] had tilted the correlation of forces—to use the Marxist argot—in our direction. Under the sway of Obama's anti-idealism, the U.S. is less interested in serving as a champion of liberty; his policies will also reduce our power, and thus our effectiveness should we choose to wield it again.

In many of Obama's performances overseas (the Nobel acceptance speech is an exception), there has been a dismaying defensiveness. It's almost as though he doesn't think we deserve to stand up for our ideals or for our interests, and believes that our record of sins, hypocrisies, and affronts makes a posture of apologetic passivity the only appropriate one. This posture raises a disturbing possibility: that the waning of America's civilizational self-confidence is part and parcel of the change Obama is effecting.

In Europe, we see a civilization that is not willing to defend itself: nations that will surrender their sovereignty, cultures that will step aside to be supplanted by an alien creed, peoples that will no longer make the most meaningful investment in the future by reproducing. There is a sense that history is over and Europeans are just waiting for someone to turn out the last light in the last gallery of the Louvre.

The Revolt Against Abandoning Exceptionalism

The popular revolt against Obama's policies is a sign that Americans are not prepared to go gentle into that good night.

Other factors are of course in play—most important, the weak economy—but the public is saying "No" to a rush to social democracy.

Although the conservatives, libertarians, and independents who oppose Obama's health-care initiative may not put it in quite these terms, they sense that his project will not just increase insurance premiums but undermine what they cherish about America. Those Americans who want to keep our detention facility at Guantanamo Bay think it necessary to protect our security—but they also worry, more profoundly, that our leaders are too apologetic to serve our interests. Americans may want change, even fundamental change, but most of them would rather change our institutions than our national character.

It is madness to consider President Obama a foreigner. But it is blindness to ignore that American exceptionalism has homegrown enemies—people who misunderstand the sources of American greatness or think them outdated. If they succeed, we will be less free, less innovative, less rich, less self-governing, and less secure. We will be less.

As will the world. The Europeans can afford a foreign policy devoted nearly exclusively to "soft power" because we are here to defend them and mount the forward defense of freedom. Who is going to do that for us, when we are no longer doing it for ourselves? Who will answer the call when America is no longer home?

If our politics seems heated right now, that is because the central question before us is whether to abandon our traditional sense of ourselves as an exceptional nation. To be exceptional is of course not to be perfect. The old anti-imperialist saying—"My country right or wrong; if right, to be kept right; if wrong, to be set right"—has considerable wisdom. But Americans are right not to want to become exceptional only in the 230-year path we took to reach the same lackluster destination as everyone else.

| *"Liberal love for the United States is
complicated by criticism."*

Belief in American
Exceptionalism Is Naïve
and Dangerous

Damon Linker

*In the following viewpoint, Damon Linker argues that American
exceptionalism tends to be defined as adherence to conservative
political principles. Linker contends that such a definition ig-
nores the volumes of social criticism from American liberals
throughout history, as well as denying the reality of US adherence to the creed of exceptionalism. The promotion of American
exceptionalism, the author argues, is ignorant and provokes opposition to America worldwide. Linker is the commentary editor
of* Newsweek/The Daily Beast *and a senior writing fellow at the
University of Pennsylvania. He is the author of* The Religious
Test: Why We Must Question the Beliefs of Our Leaders.

As you read, consider the following questions:

1. According to Linker, what country trait is unexceptional
   throughout human history?

Damon Linker, "Taking Exception," *New Republic*, February 26, 2010. Copyright © 2010
by The New Republic, Inc. All rights reserved. Reproduced by permission of *The New
Republic*.

2. According to the author, what American creed, or belief, was not open to all Americans since the founding of the country?

3. According to Linker, what traits of former President George W. Bush naturally express contemporary conservatism's outlook on the world?

Every now and then a piece of writing captures the mood of the moment and the essence of an ideology so completely that it warrants special attention. This is certainly the case with "An Exceptional Debate: The Obama Administration's Assault on American Identity," an essay (and cover story) by Richard Lowry and Ramesh Ponnuru in the March 8 [2010] issue of *National Review* [NR]. Lowry and Ponnuru's thesis—that President [Barack] Obama is an enemy of "American exceptionalism"—is hardly original. It is so widely held and so frequently asserted on the right, in fact, that it can almost be described as conservative conventional wisdom. Still, *NR*'s treatment of the subject stands out. Lowry and Ponnuru aim for comprehensiveness, and they maintain a measured, thoughtful tone throughout their essay, marshalling a wide range of historical evidence for their thesis and making well-timed concessions to contrary arguments. It's hard to imagine this key conservative claim receiving a more cogent and rhetorically effective defense. Which is precisely what makes the essay's shortcomings so striking. While its authors clearly mean it to stand as a manifesto for a resurgent conservative moment, the essay far more resembles a lullaby—a comforting compilation of consoling pieties set to a soothingly familiar melody. The perfect soundtrack to a peaceful snooze.

Exceptionalism as Conservatism

Let's begin at the beginning, with definitions. Lowry and Ponnuru aim to convince their readers that the President of the

United States denies the idea that lies at the core of American identity: that the country is exceptional. But what makes America exceptional? This is what the authors tell us: Americans affirm a creed that upholds "liberty, equality (of opportunity and respect), individualism, populism, and laissez-faire economics." These principles then combine with "other aspects of the American character—especially our religiousness and our willingness to defend ourselves by force—to form the core of American exceptionalism."

Some of this is faintly ridiculous. (Is anything less exceptional in human history than a country's willingness to defend itself by force?) As for the rest, it's either a string of American banalities and clichés—or an abstract of the Republican Party platform. The next several paragraphs of the essay make it very clear that it's the latter. That's right: Lowry and Ponnuru expect their readers to believe that what makes our country exceptional is that large numbers of Americans affirm the ideology of the modern conservative movement. But that's not quite right. Through long stretches of the essay they go much further—to imply that America is exceptional because the nation's creed *is* the ideology of the modern conservative movement.

Follow the bouncing ball: the fact that "a profit-seeking company" founded Jamestown and that Puritan merchants wrote "In the name of God and of profit" at the top of their ledgers; that, in a "telling coincidence," Adam Smith's "free-market classic" *The Wealth of Nations* was published in the same year as the Declaration of Independence; that Benjamin Franklin's name "comes from the Middle English meaning freeman, someone who owns some property"; that Abraham Lincoln supposedly hated few things more than "economic stasis"—all of these and many other anecdotes are supposed to add up to an endorsement of "the American economic gospel" (read: libertarian economic gospel) about "wealth and its creation." Meanwhile, other cherry-picked facts in later paragraphs serve to highlight the American fondness for democratic elections, the country's incorrigible patriotism and religiosity, and its "missionary impulse" to "export our model of liberty" to the world, often at the point of a gun.

Contrary American Voices

If Lowry and Ponnuru merely wished to trace the origins of several influential strands of economic and political thinking in American history—the strands that the modern conservative movement has woven into a politically potent ideological tapestry—the story they tell would be unobjectionable, if a little quirky in its emphases. But that is not their aim at all. What Lowry and Ponnuru want to accomplish is something far more pernicious—namely, to relegate contrary voices in our national narrative to the periphery of our history, and perhaps even to read them out of our history altogether.

It's a very old ideological trick—one that conservatives have mastered over the past several decades. From Allan Bloom blaming the campus violence of the 1960s on [Martin] Heidegger's *Rektoratsrede* [Rector's speech] to Sarah Palin's twangy tributes to the folksy wisdom of average Americans, it has been deployed in various idioms for various purposes over the years. But the picture it presents is always the same. On one side of an unbridgeable divide stand true Americans, devoted to God and country, liberty and virtue; on the other is an insidious assortment of liberals, leftists, radicals, secularists, and foreigners. Yes, foreigners. At its most effective, the narrative has always traced the origins of national corruption not to an aspect of American history or culture but rather to the influence of harmful foreign ideas.

That's why halfway through their essay Lowry and Ponnuru veer off on an otherwise inexplicable disquisition on European critics of the United States, which they then identify as the source of virtually any argument or political position that has diverged from the ideology of modern conservatism.

American Exceptionalism Is Un-American

"American exceptionalism"—the narcissistic soundtrack of several presidential aspirants for 2012—is Un-American. The boast betrays ignorance of the Founding Fathers and the tarnished history of the United States. In any event, to overlook faults because other nations are more flawed is juvenile, and leads nowhere.

Bruce Fein, Huffington Post, *December 17, 2010.*

[American social activist] Jane Addams, [American political philosopher] Herbert Croly, New Deal economist Stuart Chase—all of them, and many more, failed to understand and appreciate America's exceptional character and sought to replace it with "the best innovations of the modern dictatorial movements taking over in Europe" during the 1920s and '30s. That's America for you: Members of the modern conservative movement squared off against the European-inspired liberal fascists, forever searching in desperation for "a foreign template to graft onto America." If only the latter could be convinced not to hate—let alone to like or love—their country. But alas . . .

Liberalism's Aspirations

It should be clear by now where Lowry and Ponnuru believe Barack Obama's presidency has gone wrong. Instead of patriotically affirming the American exceptionalist creed—instead, that is, of governing like a Republican—he's placed our national character "under threat" and set out "to change the country fundamentally." Liberalism necessitates such radical change because liberals give their allegiance not to the country they actually inhabit but rather "to a hypothetical, pure country that is coming into being"—an ideal that looks suspiciously like the sclerotic welfare states of continental Europe. And that's the danger—that in pursuing a liberal public policy agenda, which amounts to a "rush to social democracy," the president will succeed in making us "less free, less innovative, less rich, less self-governing, and less secure"—in sum, less American. While Lowry and Ponnuru generously admit that it is "madness to consider President Obama a foreigner," they nonetheless insist that "it is blindness to ignore that American exceptionalism has homegrown enemies"—enemies such as the president of the United States.

But of course there is far more to America than is dreamt of Lowry and Ponnuru's ideologically inspired homily. Take their risible charge that liberal patriotism is defective because it sometimes puts more faith in the American future than in its past or present. Nowhere in their 5,000-word article do Lowry and Ponnuru acknowledge that significant numbers of Americans—very much including the current occupant of the White House—have very good historical reasons to feel something less than uncomplicated delight in the country's past.

The Creed of Liberty

Yes, America's principles are admirable, and the vast majority of liberals admire them deeply. But it is most certainly not the case, as Lowry and Ponnuru piously write, that America's creed of liberty—including the principle of equality of opportunity and respect—was "open to all" from the beginning. On the contrary, it was closed to many until quite recently. Indeed, it remains nearly closed to this day in the impoverished, blighted ghettos of West Philadelphia, just blocks from my office at the University of Pennsylvania, where thousands of pampered students live and study in a profoundly different world—one structured to provide them with all the knowledge and skills they'll need to take full advantage of the countless unequal opportunities that our country places before them.

Like many conservatives, Lowry and Ponnuru appear to be untroubled by the chasm that separates these two worlds. Sure, it's a source of "political tension." But it's nothing to be overly concerned about, because, they tell us, a 2003 Gallup poll showed that "31 percent of Americans expect to get rich, including 51 percent of young people and more than 20 percent of Americans making less than $30,000 year." That's right: Lowry and Ponnuru think it's a very good thing indeed that millions of Americans are deluded about their future life prospects—in fact, these senior editors of *National Review* give every indication of hoping to perpetuate the delusion.

And let's face it: they have a point. The United States would not benefit from the kind of social and political unrest that would follow from the shattering of its citizens' economic pipe dreams. Conservatives like Lowry and Ponnuru respond to this fact by upholding the fiction that America has always been a land of equal opportunity for all. Liberals respond by crafting policies that they hope will bring the country into closer conformity to the ideal of equal opportunity for all. That's one way to define the division of labor that separates our nation's parties at this moment in our history. What should disgust all historically informed citizens is the smarmy and ignorant insinuation that the liberal response—the one that seeks to make the United States a fairer and freer nation for more of its citizens—is something less than authentically American.

A Naïve Belief in Superiority

Lowry and Ponnuru are right about one thing: liberal love for the United States is complicated by criticism. And that appears to be something the right simply cannot abide, or perhaps even understand. How else to explain the bizarre passage of their essay in which Lowry and Ponnuru slam President Obama for failing to "defend the country's honor" when a foreign critic "brought up the Bay of Pigs" during an overseas trip? Apparently "acknowledging that America has been a force for good" in the world, as Obama did, is not enough. The man who leads the nation that is by almost any measure indisputably the most powerful on earth must go further—to make a fool of himself and the country by defending an escapade from half-a-century ago that nearly everyone acknowledges was an embarrassing blunder. But that's not all. According to Lowry and Ponnuru, he must also robustly defend American exceptionalism—and thus American moral superiority—before foreign audiences, evidently because it's the president's duty to provoke anger and resentment, and thus opposition to our global leadership, around the world.

Lots of conservatives turned on George W. Bush by the end of his presidency. But here we see that if Bush didn't exist, the right would have had to invent him. His proud parochialism, his simple-minded and insecure suspicion of intelligence, his swaggering self-righteousness—all of it is the natural expression of contemporary conservatism's outlook on the world.

Alexis de Tocqueville, a hero to many on the right, noted with concern nearly two centuries ago that Americans were prone to "the perpetual utterance of self-applause." For all of his prescience, I suspect the great Frenchman would be surprised and disappointed to find that all these years later, at a time when the country faces daunting long-term challenges, one of the nation's two governing ideologies has come to define itself by its singular dedication to the proposition that the standing ovation never stop.

"American leadership must be re-focused
toward partnership."

American Leadership
in the World Should
Involve Partnership

Bruce Jones, Carlos Pascual, and Stephen John Stedman

In the following viewpoint, Bruce Jones, Carlos Pascual, and Stephen John Stedman argue that unprecedented interdependence created by globalization means that it is in the interest of the United States to engage in responsible sovereignty, recognizing obligations toward other countries. The authors contend that increased global partnership is necessary for the United States to be an effective world leader. Jones is director and senior fellow of the New York University Center on International Cooperation and director of the Managing Global Order Program at the Brookings Institution. Pascual is US ambassador to Mexico. Stedman is a senior fellow at Stanford University Center for International Security and Cooperation.

Bruce Jones, Carlos Pascual, and Stephen John Stedman, *A Plan for Action: A New Era of International Cooperation for a Changed World: 2009, 2010, and Beyond*, Managing Global Insecurity (now known as Managing Global Order Project, a project of Center on International Cooperation, New York University; Brookings Institution; and Center for International Security and Cooperation, Stanford University), September 2008, pp. 10–14. Reproduced by permission.

As you read, consider the following questions:

1. The authors suggest that the United States needs to cultivate new partnerships with what four countries?

2. The authors point to a 2007 poll that showed what percentage of voters favoring a president who would share the burden of promoting peace in the world?

3. The authors cite a 2008 poll that showed that which two US allies had extensive concerns that US foreign policy does not take into account the interests of other countries?

The greatest test of global leadership in the 21st century will be how nations perform in the face of threats that defy borders—from nuclear proliferation, conflict, and climate change to terrorism, threats to biological security, and global poverty. Ours is now a world where national security is interdependent with global security.

National and Global Security

Globalization has resulted in unprecedented opportunities. The ability to tap into global markets for capital, technology and labor has allowed the private sector to amass wealth unfathomable 50 years ago: it has helped lift hundreds of millions out of poverty in emerging economies. For China, integration into the global economy has been the driver of one of the most remarkable stories of national progress in human history—500 million people have been raised out of poverty in just thirty years.

Yet, the forces of globalization that have stitched the world together and driven prosperity can also tear it apart. In the face of new transnational threats and profound security interdependence, even the strongest nations depend on the cooperation of others to protect their own national security. No country, including the United States, is capable of successfully meeting the challenges, or capitalizing on the opportunities, of this changed world alone. It is a world for which we are unprepared, a world that poses a challenge to leaders and citizens alike to redefine their interests and re-examine their responsibilities. While that is true of every country, it is especially true of the most powerful—which must exercise the most responsibility.

U.S. foreign policy has lagged behind these realities. A new approach is needed to revitalize the alliances, diplomacy, and international institutions central to the inseparable relationship between national and global security.

U.S. leadership is indispensable if the world as a whole is to be successful in managing today's threats. But American leadership must be re-focused toward partnership—continuing partnership with allies in Europe, Asia and Latin America, and cultivating new partnerships with rising powers such as China, India, Brazil and South Africa. The policies, attitudes, and actions of major states will have disproportionate influence on whether the next 50 years tend to international order or entropy [meaning chaos or disorder]. The actions of a new U.S. President, working with the leaders of the traditional and rising powers, will profoundly influence the shape of international security and prosperity for a global age.

A Common Vision

Unprecedented interdependence does not make international cooperation inevitable. Rather, shared interests must be translated into a common vision for a revitalized international security system that benefits all.

Foresight, imagination, pragmatism and political commitment, fueled by effective American leadership, created a new international era after World War II. Institutions such as the United Nations, the International Monetary Fund, the World Bank and the General Agreement on Tariffs and Trade (now the World Trade Organization) contributed to extraordinary economic growth and helped to prevent major-power war. Innovation and political engagement on the same scale are needed to achieve security and prosperity in the years ahead.

However, the vision necessary for a 21st century international security system is clouded by a mismatch between existing post-World War II multilateral institutions premised on *traditional sovereignty*—a belief that borders are sacrosanct and an insistence on non-interference in domestic affairs— and the realities of a now transnational world where capital, technology, labor, disease, pollution and non-state actors traverse boundaries irrespective of the desires of sovereign states.

The domestic burdens inflicted by transnational threats such as poverty, civil war, disease and environmental degradation point in one direction: toward cooperation with global partners and a strengthening of international institutions. Entering agreements or accepting assistance is not a weakening of sovereignty; it is the exercise of sovereignty in order to protect it.

A Principle of Responsible Sovereignty

The MGI [Managing Global Insecurity] Project's consultations have informed and validated the view that a new era of international cooperation should be built on the principle of *responsible sovereignty*: the idea that states must take responsibility for the external effects of their domestic actions—that sovereignty entails obligations and duties towards other sovereign states as well as to one's own citizens. To protect national security, even to protect sovereignty, states must negotiate rules and norms to guide actions that reverberate beyond national boundaries. Responsible sovereignty also implies a positive interest on the part of powerful states to provide weaker states with the capacity to exercise their sovereignty responsibly—a *responsibility to build*.

Impressions Among American Voters

	Mean Rating
America Doing Its Fair Share Around the World	66
International Cooperation	66
Global Partnerships	63
International Burden-Sharing	58
Multilateralism	49
America Going It Alone	38
Isolationism	30

"For each term, please rate your overall impression of the term, using a scale of zero to one hundred, where zero means you have a very unfavorable opinion of the term and one hundred means you have a very favorable opinion of the term and fifty is neutral. You can use any number between zero and one hundred depending on your overall feeling or impression of the term."

TAKEN FROM: *Public Opinion Strategies & Hart Research,* UNF Research/August 2008.

MGI emphasizes sovereignty because states are still the primary units of the international system. As much as globalization has diminished the power of states, there is simply no alternative to the legally defined state as the primary actor in international affairs nor is there any substitute for state legitimacy in the use of force, the provision of justice, and the regulation of public spheres and private action.

MGI emphasizes responsibility because, in an era of globalization, adherence to *traditional sovereignty,* and deference to individual state solutions, have failed to produce peace and prosperity. In a transnational world, international cooperation is essential to give states the means to meet the most fundamental demands of sovereignty: to protect their people and advance their interests.

Responsible sovereignty, in sum, is a guidepost to a better international system. Just as the founders of the United Nations and Bretton Woods institutions began with a vision for international cooperation based on a shared assessment of threat and a shared notion of sovereignty, today's global powers must chart a new course for today's greatest challenges and opportunities.

A Declining US Image

A new vision for global security will only succeed if it is powered by political commitment and has the support of diverse regions and influential constituencies. International politics and global realities are converging to make such cooperation possible.

In the United States, MGI consultations with policymakers and recent polling highlight that American citizens and American leadership across party lines are concerned with a declining U.S. image internationally.

In a 2007 national poll, 81% of Americans favored a Presidential candidate who said the United States should "share the burden" and not be the sole supplier of resources, finances, military forces, and diplomacy for peace in the world. Americans polled rejected "going it alone," and believed the United States should be a global leader and a "role model" for democracy. Presidential candidates have mirrored this bipartisan public sentiment: both major candidates [John McCain (R) and Barack Obama (D)] have spoken out for restoring U.S. leadership and moral standing, viewing this as critical to the protection of U.S. security.

The Need for Global Partners

The next U.S. President has the opportunity to feature international cooperation as the centerpiece of a strategy to restore America's global leadership. Americans want their country to be respected, they want to lead, and they want to feel more secure as a result of U.S. engagement.

Just as important, current global realities leave no alternative to cooperation. On January 20, 2009, the next American

President will inherit crises in Iraq, Iran, Afghanistan, North Korea, Darfur, Pakistan, and the Middle East. There will be many regional and national challenges to a viable foreign policy: the rise of India and China, an energy-brash Russia, and an African continent caught between new economic opportunities and a legacy of conflict and failed governance. The international community will demand action on climate change and the global food crisis. An American recession will focus attention on vulnerabilities in the global financial system. Key U.S. allies will seek renewed U.S. commitment to multilateralism.

The United States cannot retreat from this agenda any more than it can manage it alone. America needs global partners: to combat threats to the American people, to wield influence with actors such as North Korea and Iran, to share the burden on complex challenges, and to sustain global systems that allow the United States access to capital and markets critical to economic growth in a dismal domestic budget environment. It is in America's self-interest to act now, while its influence is strong, to model leadership for the 21st century based on the premise of partnership and recognition of interdependence.

US Power and Leadership

MGI consultations in key capitals in diverse regions—from Beijing and Delhi to London and Doha [Qatar]—reinforced that unilateral U.S. action in Iraq, and across a range of foreign policy issues, has cast a long shadow on America's standing in the world and alienated even close allies. Key international stakeholders are eager for strong signals from a new U.S. administration that it is willing to re-value global partnerships and re-commit the United States to a rules-based international system.

International public opinion polls reinforce this sentiment. Of more than 24,000 people across 24 countries surveyed in

March and April 2008, a majority expressed negative views of the role that the United States is playing in the world. In 14 of 24 countries, two-thirds or more of respondents expressed little or no confidence in President [George W.] Bush to do the right thing in world affairs. The belief that the United States does not take into account the interests of other countries in formulating its foreign policy is extensive even among U.S. allies such as the UK and Australia and overwhelming in the Middle East and Asia.

Yet, internationally, most policymakers also still recognize that there is no prospect for international security and prosperity in the next 20 years that does not rely heavily on U.S. power and leadership. The United States has the world's largest economy, strongest military and broadest alliances. The world needs the United States to use its leadership and resources for the resolution of transnational threats. If the United States blocks international solutions on issues such as climate change, nuclear security and financial stability, sustainable global outcomes are unachievable.

A Convergence of Interests

Traditional and emerging powers also share with the United States a self-interest in a resilient and effective international order. Europe is the world's most rule-based society, yet erosion of a rule-based international system means that Europe is taking on commitments, such as on carbon emissions and foreign aid, with increasingly marginal impact. Japan has a vital interest in a stable transition in security arrangements in Asia and globally. Leaders in China, India and the emerging economies recognize that their economic growth relies on a strong and resilient international trade and finance system. To continue to develop its oil and gas reserves, Russia will need international technology, and sufficient trust from its partners to invest in and secure transnational pipelines. None of the traditional or rising powers profits from unchecked prolifera-tion, or the spread of global terrorism.

We must capitalize on momentum generated from a con-vergence of global and U.S. domestic interests to build an in-ternational security system for the 21st century. The case for amplified international cooperation is not a soft-hearted ap-peal to the common good but rather a realist call to action that is demanded both domestically and internationally.

> "'Sharing' sovereignty . . . will diminish the sovereign power of the American people over their government and their own lives."

America Should Not Share Sovereignty with Other Nations

John Bolton

In the following viewpoint, John Bolton contends that the suggestion that the United States should share or give up any of its national sovereignty is misguided. Bolton claims that diplomacy should not be an end in itself. He also rejects the idea that multilateralism should be embraced over unilateralism, expressing concern about the degree of sovereignty that the United States might give up by embracing international standards. Bolton is a senior fellow at the American Enterprise Institute, former US permanent representative to the United Nations (2005–2006), and former under secretary of state for arms control and international security (2001–2005). He is the author of Surrender Is Not an Option.

As you read, consider the following questions:

1. Bolton claims that Americans historically have understood sovereignty to mean what?

2. The author claims that diplomacy does not work without the threat of what three things?

3. What three votes by the United Nations (UN) does Bolton give as examples of issues where international standards are not appropriate?

Barack Obama's nascent presidency has brought forth the customary flood of policy proposals from the great and good, all hoping to influence his administration. One noteworthy offering is a short report with a distinguished provenance titled *A Plan for Action*, which features a revealingly immodest subtitle: *A New Era of International Cooperation for a Changed World: 2009, 2010, and Beyond.*

In presentation and tone, *A Plan for Action* is determinedly uncontroversial; indeed, it looks and reads more like a corporate brochure than a foreign-policy paper. The text is the work of three academics—Bruce Jones of NYU [New York University], Carlos Pascual of the Brookings Institution, and Stephen John Stedman of Stanford [University]. Its findings and recommendations, they claim, rose from a series of meetings with foreign-policy eminences here and abroad, including former Secretaries of State of both parties as well as defense officials from the [Bill] Clinton and first [George H.W.] Bush administrations. The participation of these notables is what gives *A Plan for Action* its bona fides, though one should doubt how much the document actually reflects their ideas. There is no question, however, that the ideas advanced in *A Plan for Action* have become mainstays in the liberal vision of the future of American foreign policy.

That is what makes *A Plan for Action* especially interesting, and especially worrisome. If it is what it appears to be—a blueprint for the Obama administration's effort to construct a foreign policy different from George W. Bush's—then the nation's governing elite is in the process of taking a sharp, indeed radical, turn away from the principles and practices of representative self-government that have been at the core of the American experiment since the nation's founding. The pivot point is a shifting understanding of American sovereignty.

The Definition of Sovereignty

While the term "sovereignty" has acquired many, often inconsistent, definitions, Americans have historically understood it to mean our collective right to govern ourselves within our Constitutional framework. Today's liberal elite, by contrast, sees sovereignty as something much more abstract and less tangible, and thus a prize of less value to individual citizens than it once might have been. They argue that the model accepted by European countries in the Peace of Westphalia in 1648, which assigned to individual nation-states the right and responsibility to manage their own affairs within their own borders, is in the process of being superseded by new structures more appropriate to the 21st century.

In this regard, they usually cite the European Union (EU) as the new model, with its 27 member nations falling under the aegis of a centralized financial system administered in Brussels. On issue after issue, from climate change to trade, American liberals increasingly look to Europe's example of transnational consensus as the proper model for the United States. That is particularly true when it comes to national security, as [Senator] John Kerry revealed when, during his presidential bid in 2004, he said that American policy had to pass a "global test" in order to secure its legitimacy.

This is not a view with which the broader American population has shown much comfort. Traditionally, Americans have resisted the notion that their government's actions had to pass muster with other governments, often with widely differing values and interests. It is the foreign-policy establishment's unease with this long-held American conviction that is the motivating factor behind *A Plan for Action*, which represents a bold attempt to argue that any such set of beliefs has simply been overtaken by events.

The Call for Responsible Sovereignty

To this end, the authors provide a brief for what they call "responsible sovereignty." They define it as "the notion that sovereignty entails obligations and duties toward other states as well as to one's own citizens," and they believe that its application can form the basis for a "cooperative international order." At first glance, the phrase "responsible sovereignty" may seem unremarkable, given the paucity of advocates for "irresponsible sovereignty." But despite the *Plan*'s mainstream provenance, the conception is a dramatic overhaul of sovereignty itself.

"Global leaders," the *Plan* insists, "increasingly recognize that alone they are unable to protect their interests and their citizens—national security has become interdependent with global security." The United States must therefore commit to "a rule-based international system that rejects unilateralism and looks beyond military might," or else "resign [our]selves to an ad-hoc international system." Mere "traditional sovereignty" is insufficient in the new era we have entered, an era in which we must contend with "the realities of a now transnational world." This "rule-based international system" will create the conditions for "global governance."

The *Plan* suggests that the transition to this new system must begin immediately because of the terrible damage done by the [George W.] Bush administration. In the *Plan*'s narrative, Bush disdained diplomacy, uniformly preferring the use of force, regime change, preemptive attacks, and general swagger in its conduct of foreign affairs. The *Plan*, by contrast, "rejects unilateralism and looks beyond military might." Its implementation will lead to the successful resolution of dispute after dispute and usher in a new and unprecedented period of worldwide comity.

The Utility of Diplomacy

As the Obama years begin, we certainly do need a lively debate on the utility of diplomacy, but it would be better if that debate were not conducted on the false premise offered by *A Plan for Action*. In reality, in the overwhelming majority of cases, foreign-policy thinkers on both sides of the ideological divide believe diplomacy is the solution to the difficulties that arise in the international system. That is how the [George W.] Bush administration conducted itself as well.

The difference arises in the consideration of a tiny number of cases—cases that prove entirely resistant to diplomatic efforts, in which divergent national interests prove implacably resistant to reconciliation. If diplomacy does not and cannot work, the continued application of it to a problematic situation is akin to subjecting a cancer patient to a regimen of chemotherapy that shows no results whatever. The result may look like treatment, but it is, in fact, only making the patient sicker and offering no possibility of improvement.

Diplomacy is like all other human activity. It has costs and it has benefits. Whether to engage in diplomacy on a given matter requires a judicious assessment of both costs and benefits. This is an exercise about which reasonable people can disagree. If diplomacy is to work, it must be preceded by an effort to determine its parameters—when it might be best to begin, how to achieve one's aims, and what the purpose of the process might be. At the cold war's outset, for example, [President] Harry Truman's Secretary of State, Dean Acheson, frequently observed that he was prepared to negotiate with the Soviets only when America could do so from a position of strength.

The Issue of Time

Time is one of the most important variables in a diplomatic dance, because it often imposes a cost on one side and a benefit to its adversary. Nations can use the time granted by a diplomatic process to obscure their objectives, build alliances, prepare operationally for war, and, especially today, accelerate their efforts to build weapons of mass destruction and the ballistic missiles that might carry them. There are concrete economic factors that must be considered as well in the act of seeking to engage an adversary in the diplomatic realm—the act of providing humanitarian assistance as an act of good will, for example, the suspension of economic sanctions, or even resuming normal trade relations during negotiations.

Obviously, the United States and, indeed, all rational nations are entirely comfortable paying substantial costs when they appear to be wise investments that will lead to the achievement of a larger objective. Alas, such happy conclusions are far from inevitable, and failing to understand the truth of this uncomfortable and inarguable reality has led nations to prolong negotiations long after the last glimmer of progress has been snuffed out. For too many diplomats, there is no off switch for diplomacy, no moment at which the only sensible thing to do is rise from the table and go home.

Has one ever heard of a diplomat working to fashion an "exit strategy" from a failed negotiation? One hasn't. One should.

Diplomacy as an End in Itself

Diplomacy is a tool, not a policy. It is a technique, not an end in itself. Urging, however earnestly, that we "engage" with our enemies tells us nothing about what happens after concluding the initial pleasantries at the negotiating table. Just opening the conversation is often significant, especially for those who are legitimized merely by being present. But without more, the meaning and potency of the photo op will quickly fade.

That is why effective diplomacy must be one aspect of a larger strategic spectrum that includes ugly and public confrontations. Without the threat of painful sanctions, harsh condemnations, and even the use of force, diplomacy risks becoming a sucker's game, in which one side will sit forever in naïve hope of reaching a settlement while the other side acts at will.

Diplomacy is an end in itself in *A Plan for Action*. So, too, is multilateralism. The multilateralism the *Plan* celebrates and advocates is, of course, set in sharp contrast to the portrait it draws of a Bush administration flush with unilateralist cowboys intent on overturning existing international treaties and institutions just for the sport of it. Defining unilateralism is straightforward: the word refers to a state acting on its own in international affairs. It is a critical conceptual mistake, however, to pose "multilateralism" simply as its opposite.

The Multilateralism of International Organizations

Consider, for example, the various roles of the United Nations [UN], the North Atlantic Treaty Organization [NATO], and the Proliferation Security Initiative. The UN, the Holy Grail of multilateralism, is an organization of 192 members with responsibility for the maintenance of international peace and security lodged in its Security Council. NATO is a defense alliance of 26 states, all of which are Western democracies. The Proliferation Security Initiative (PSI), created in 2003 by the Bush administration, now includes 90-plus diverse countries dedicated to stopping international trafficking in weapons of mass destruction.

Each organization is clearly "multilateral," but their roles are so wildly different that the word ceases to have any meaning. For example, if the United States confronted a serious threat, it would be acting multilaterally if it took the matter either to NATO or the UN. Both options would be "multilateral," but widely divergent in diplomatic and political content, and quite likely in military significance as well. They would be comparably related in the same way a steak knife is comparable to a plastic butter knife.

The PSI offers an even starker contrast, for unlike either the UN or NATO, it has no secretary general, no Secretariat, no headquarters, and no regularly scheduled meetings. One British diplomat described the initiative as "an activity, not an organization." In fact, the model of the Proliferation Security Initiative is the ideal one for multilateral activity in the future, precisely because it transcends the traditional structures of international organizations, which have, time and again, proved inefficient and ineffective.

"Multilateralism" is, in other words, merely a word that describes international action taken by a group of nations acting in concert. For the authors of *A Plan for Action*, however, multilateralism has an almost spiritual aspect, representing a harmony that transcends barriers and oceans.

Harmony Through International Standards

Harmony is designed to stifle any discordant notes, and so is the multilateralism envisioned by an American foreign policy guided by "responsible sovereignty." It is one in which the group of nations, of which the United States is but a single player among many, initiates policies and activities that would likely be designed to constrain the freedom of action of the United States in pursuit of that harmony—not only in its activities abroad, but also in its activities within the 50 states.

There is a precedent for this in the conduct of the European Union, whose 27 nations now possess a common currency in the form of the euro and an immensely complex series of trade and labor policies intended to cut across sovereign lines. The EU is the model *A Plan for Action* proffers for the "responsible sovereignty" regime its authors wish to import to the United States. EU bureaucrats based in Brussels have been reshaping the priorities and needs of EU member states for a decade now, and proposing a system based on the design of the EU suggests a desire to subject the United States to a kind of international oversight not only when it comes to foreign policy but also on matters properly understood as U.S. domestic policy.

That very approach has been on display at the United Nations for years in an effort to standardize international conduct that has come to be known as "norming." In theory, there is good reason to create international standards—for measurement, for example, or for conduct on the high seas. But "norming" goes far beyond such prosaic concerns. The UN has, for example, repeatedly voted in different committees to condemn the death penalty, in a clear effort to put pressure on the United States to follow suit. Similar votes have been taken on abortion rights and restricting the private ownership of firearms.

The Danger of Sharing Sovereignty

Such issues have been, and likely will again be, the subjects of intense democratic debate within the United States, and properly so. There is no need to internationalize them to make the debate more fruitful. What is common to these and many other issues is that the losers in our domestic debate are often the proponents of internationalizing the controversies. They think that if they can change the political actors, they can change the political outcome. Unsuccessful in our domestic political arena, they seek to redefine the arena in which these matters will be adjudicated—moving, in effect, from unilateral, democratic U.S. decision-making to a multilateral, bureaucratic, and elitist environment. For almost any domestic issue one can imagine, there are likely to be nongovernmental organizations roaming the international arena desperately trying to turn their priorities into "norming" issues.

This is what "responsible sovereignty" would look like. For the authors and signatories of *A Plan of Action*, sovereignty is simply an abstraction, a historical concept about as important today as the "sovereigns" from whose absolute rights the term originally derived. That is not the understanding of the U.S. Constitution, which locates the basis of its legitimacy in "we the people," who constitute the sovereign authority of the nation.

"Sharing" sovereignty with someone or something else is thus not abstract for Americans. Doing so by definition will diminish the sovereign power of the American people over their government and their own lives, the very purpose for which the Constitution was written. This is something Americans have been reluctant to do. Now their reluctance may have to take the form of more concerted action against "responsible sovereignty" if its onward march is to be halted or reversed. Our Founders would clearly understand the need.

Periodical and Internet Sources Bibliography

The following articles have been selected to supplement the diverse views presented in this chapter.

John R. Bolton — "Should the United States Act with Humility in International Affairs? No," *In Character*, Winter 2010.

Chalmers Johnson — "Three Good Reasons to Liquidate Our Empire," *Nation*, August 17, 2009.

Robert D. Kaplan — "The Revenge of Geography," *Foreign Policy*, May/June 2009. www.foreignpolicy.com.

Lawrence J. Korb — "Should the United States Act with Humility in International Affairs? Yes," *In Character*, Winter 2010.

Joel Kotkin — "Undying Creed: The Acceleration of Our Exceptionalism," *World Affairs*, January/February 2010.

Catherine Lutz — "Obama's Empire," *New Statesman*, August 3, 2009. www.newstatesman.com.

Mark Mazower — "Saviors & Sovereigns: The Rise and Fall of Humanitarianism," *World Affairs*, March/April 2010. www.worldaffairsjournal.org.

John J. Mearsheimer — "Imperial by Design," *National Interest*, January/February 2011.

Paul R. Pillar — "The Errors of Exceptionalism," *National Interest*, November 30, 2010.

Paul Wolfowitz — "Obama and the Freedom Agenda," *Wall Street Journal*, June 3, 2009.

Fareed Zakaria — "Why Washington Worries," *Newsweek*, March 14, 2009.

OPPOSING
VIEWPOINTS®
SERIES

CHAPTER 2

Is US Military Intervention Around the Globe Good for America?

Chapter Preface

The United States has a long history of overseas military intervention. To date, the two most significant US military interventions of the twenty-first century are the wars in Iraq and Afghanistan, which have caused criticism both within the United States and abroad. The 2010 Pew Research Center's Global Attitudes Project found that the majority of countries surveyed believe that the United States should remove troops from Afghanistan. One frequent criticism of the United States is that it acts unilaterally, or by itself, in taking military action against other countries. This criticism was particularly acute at the start of the Iraq war.

A policy of unilateralism is one in which a country conducts its foreign affairs in a one-sided manner, with little consultation or involvement with other countries. By contrast, a policy of multilateralism is one in which a country conducts its foreign affairs in a way that seeks the endorsement and involvement of other countries. The United Nations (UN), founded in 1945, is the main international body that seeks to maintain international peace and cooperation through the use of multilateral policy. The United States is one of the 192 member states in the organization. The UN Security Council is in charge of maintaining international peace and security, consisting of 15 member states, including the United States, which is one of the Council's five permanent members.

In response to the US government's claim that Iraq was developing weapons of mass destruction (WMDs), in November 2002 the UN Security Council passed Resolution 1441, which called for Iraq to allow UN weapons inspectors to search for WMDs. The UN found no evidence of WMDs and was confident in disarmament by continued inspections, but before the Security Council finished inspection, the United States and United Kingdom invaded Iraq in March 2003, without the support of the UN Security Council. This unilateral invasion caused much outcry in the international community. In September 2004, UN Secretary General Kofi Annan told BBC news he believed that from the point of view of the UN charter the invasion of Iraq was illegal.

Although President George W. Bush and his supporters allege that the perceived danger of WMDs in Iraq justified unilateral action, critics both within the United States and outside decried the action. The critics' argument became even stronger when WMDs were never discovered during the war. Regardless of the status of WMDs, the unilateral action itself damaged the reputation of the United States as a team player in the United Nations and other international organizations. President Barack Obama laid out a new national security strategy in May 2010 that appeared to diverge from the unilateralist strategy of President Bush to some extent. "America has not succeeded by stepping outside the currents of international cooperation" and "we will seek broad international support, working with such institutions as NATO [North Atlantic Treaty Organization] and the UN Security Council," Obama said. But he also notes, "The United States must reserve the right to act unilaterally if necessary to defend our nation and our interests." If the United States does take unilateral military action in the future, however, the country is likely to face critics.

| *"It is always tempting to believe that the international order the United States built and sustained with its power can exist in the absence of that power."* |

US Military Power Must Be Maintained for Current and Future Interventions

Robert Kagan

In the following viewpoint, Robert Kagan argues that US defense spending needs to be free from budget cuts in order to maintain strong US military power. Kagan claims that especially with the high risks faced internationally, reducing US military interventions could be dangerous. He claims that the United States and the rest of the world have benefitted from past US military interventions, and that there are many situations worldwide that may need US military intervention in the future. Kagan is a senior fellow of foreign policy at the Brookings Institution, and he is a contributing editor at the Weekly Standard *and the* New Republic.

As you read, consider the following questions:

1. Kagan claims that US military actions in what four countries make it difficult for terrorists to plan and carry out attacks against Americans on US soil?

2. The author argues that the only way to gain significant savings from US defense spending is to do what?

3. Kagan claims that the United States has undertaken roughly how many overseas interventions since 1898?

The looming battle over the defense budget could produce a useful national discussion about American foreign and defense policy. But we would need to begin by dispensing with the most commonly repeated fallacy: that cutting defense is essential to restoring the nation's fiscal health. People can be forgiven for believing this myth, given how often they hear it. Typical is a recent *Foreign Affairs* article [by Gordon Adams and Matthew Leatherman] claiming that the United States faces "a watershed moment" and "must decide whether to increase its already massive debt in order to continue being the world's sheriff or restrain its military missions and focus on economic recovery."

The Arguments for Cutting US Defense Spending

This is nonsense. No serious budget analyst or economist believes that cutting the defense budget will aid economic recovery in the near term—federal spending on defense is just as much a job-producing stimulus as federal spending on infrastructure. Nor, more importantly, do they believe that cutting defense spending will have more than the most marginal effect on reducing the runaway deficits projected for the coming years. The simple fact is, as my Brookings [Institution] colleague and former budget czar Alice Rivlin recently observed, the scary projections of future deficits are *not* "caused by rising defense spending," and even if one assumes that defense spending continues to increase with the rate of inflation, this is "not what's driving the future spending." The engine of our growing debt is entitlements.

So why are the various commissions, including the Rivlin-Domenici commission, as well as members of Congress, calling for defense cuts at all? The answer boils down to one of fairness, and politics. It is not that cutting defense is necessary to save the economy. But if the American people are going to be asked to accept cuts in their domestic entitlements, the assumption runs, they're going to want to see the pain shared across the board, including by defense.

This "fair share" argument is at least more sober than phony "cut defense or kill the economy" sensationalism, and it has the appearance of reasonableness. But it is still based on a fallacy. Distributing cuts equally is not an intrinsically good thing. If you wanted to reduce the gas consumption of your gas-guzzling car by 10 percent, you wouldn't remove 10 percent of your front and rear bumpers so that all parts of the car shared the pain. The same goes for the federal budget. Not all cuts have equal effect on the national well-being. Few would propose cutting spending on airport security, for instance. At a time of elevated risk of terrorist attack, we don't need to show the American people that airport security is contributing its "fair share" to budget reduction.

The International Situation

Today the international situation is also one of high risk.

- The terrorists who would like to kill Americans on U.S. soil constantly search for safe havens from which to plan and carry out their attacks. American military actions in Afghanistan, Pakistan, Iraq, Yemen, and elsewhere make it harder for them to strike and are a large part of the reason why for almost a decade there has been no repetition of September 11. To the degree that we limit our ability to deny them safe haven, we increase the chances they will succeed.

- American forces deployed in East Asia and the Western Pacific have for decades prevented the outbreak of major war, provided stability, and kept open international trading routes, making possible an unprecedented era of growth and prosperity for Asians and Americans alike. Now the United States faces a new challenge and potential threat from a rising China which seeks eventually to push the U.S. military's area of operations back to Hawaii and exercise hegemony over the world's most rapidly growing economies. Meanwhile, a nuclear-armed North Korea threatens war with South Korea and fires ballistic missiles over Japan that will someday be capable of reaching the west coast of the United States. Democratic nations in the region, worried that the United States may be losing influence, turn to Washington for reassurance that the U.S. security guarantee remains firm. If the United States cannot provide that assurance because it is cutting back its military capabilities, they will have to choose between accepting Chinese dominance and striking out on their own, possibly by building nuclear weapons.

- In the Middle East, Iran seeks to build its own nuclear arsenal, supports armed radical Islamic groups in Lebanon and Palestine, and has linked up with anti-American dictatorships in the Western Hemisphere. The prospects of new instability in the region grow every day as a decrepit regime in Egypt clings to power, crushes all moderate opposition, and drives the Muslim Brotherhood into the streets. A nuclear-armed Pakistan seems to be ever on the brink of collapse into anarchy and radicalism. Turkey, once an ally, now seems bent on an increasingly anti-American Islamist course. The prospect of war between Hezbollah and Israel grows, and with it the possibility of war between Israel and Syria and possibly Iran. There, too, nations in the region increasingly look to Washington for reassurance, and if they decide the United States cannot be relied upon they will have to decide whether to succumb to Iranian influence or build their own nuclear weapons to resist it.

The Danger of Reduced Interventions

In the 1990s, after the Soviet Union had collapsed and the biggest problem in the world seemed to be ethnic conflict in the Balkans, it was at least plausible to talk about cutting back on American military capabilities. In the present, increasingly dangerous international environment, in which terrorism and great power rivalry vie as the greatest threat to American security and interests, cutting military capacities is simply reckless. Would we increase the risk of strategic failure in an already risky world, despite the near irrelevance of the defense budget to American fiscal health, just so we could tell American voters that their military had suffered its "fair share" of the pain?

The nature of the risk becomes plain when one considers the nature of the cuts that would have to be made to have even a marginal effect on the U.S. fiscal crisis. Many are under the illusion, for instance, that if the United States simply withdrew from Iraq and Afghanistan and didn't intervene anywhere else for a while, this would have a significant impact on future deficits. But, in fact, projections of future massive deficits already assume the winding down of these interventions. Withdrawal from the two wars would scarcely make a dent in the fiscal crisis. Nor can meaningful reductions be achieved by cutting back on waste at the Pentagon—which Secretary of Defense [Robert] Gates has already begun to do and which

The Importance of US Power

Ever since the end of World War II, American power has been the chief deterrent to aggression: the shield under which the tools of diplomacy, trade, and engagement have produced unprecedented progress toward freedom and democracy. But the shield is cracking. America's global influence is being checked and rolled back, and even the homeland is no longer safe from attack.

James Talent, "A Constitutional Basis for Defense,"
America at Risk Memo, June 1, 2010.

has also been factored into deficit projections. If the United States withdrew from Iran and Afghanistan tomorrow, cut all the waste Gates can find, and even eliminated a few weapons programs—all this together would still not produce a 10 percent decrease in overall defense spending.

In fact, the only way to get significant savings from the defense budget—and by "significant," we are still talking about a tiny fraction of the cuts needed to bring down future deficits—is to cut force structure: fewer troops on the ground; fewer airplanes in the skies; fewer ships in the water; fewer soldiers, pilots, and sailors to feed and clothe and provide benefits for. To cut the size of the force, however, requires reducing or eliminating the missions those forces have been performing. Of course, there are any number of think tank experts who insist U.S. forces can be cut by a quarter or third or even by half and still perform those missions. But this is snake oil. Over the past two decades, the force has already been cut by a third. Yet no administration has reduced the missions that the larger force structures of the past were designed to meet. To fulfill existing security commitments, to remain the "world's power balancer of choice," as [author] Leslie Gelb puts it, to act as "the only regional balancer against China in Asia, Russia in eastern Europe, and Iran in the Middle East" requires at least the current force structure, and almost certainly more than current force levels. Those who recommend doing the same with less are only proposing a policy of insufficiency, where the United States makes commitments it cannot meet except at high risk of failure. . . .

The Benefits of US Military Interventions

Whatever the nature of the current economic difficulties, the past six decades have seen a greater increase in global prosperity than any time in human history. Hundreds of millions have been lifted out of poverty. Once-backward nations have become economic dynamos. And the American economy, though suffering ups and downs throughout this period, has on the whole benefited immensely from this international order. One price of this success has been maintaining a sufficient military capacity to provide the essential security underpinnings of this order. But has the price not been worth it? In the first half of the 20th century, the United States found itself engaged in two world wars. In the second half, this global American strategy helped produce a peaceful end to the greatpower struggle of the Cold War and then 20 more years of great-power peace. Looked at coldly, simply in terms of dollars and cents, the benefits of that strategy far outweigh the costs.

The danger, as always, is that we don't even realize the benefits our strategic choices have provided. Many assume that the world has simply become more peaceful, that greatpower conflict has become impossible, that nations have learned that military force has little utility, that economic power is what counts. This belief in progress and the perfectibility of humankind and the institutions of international order is always alluring to Americans and Europeans and other children of the Enlightenment. It was the prevalent belief in the decade before World War I, in the first years after World War II, and in those heady days after the Cold War when people spoke of the "end of history." It is always tempting to believe that the international order the United States built and sustained with its power can exist in the absence of that power, or at least with much less of it. This is the hidden assumption of those who call for a change in American strategy: that the United States can stop playing its role and yet all the benefits that came from that role will keep pouring in. This is a great if recurring illusion, the idea that you can pull a leg out from under a table and the table will not fall over.

Much of the present debate, it should be acknowledged, is not about the defense budget or the fiscal crisis at all. It is only the latest round in a long-running debate over the nature and purposes of American foreign policy. At the tactical level, some use the fiscal crisis as a justification for a different approach to, say, Afghanistan. Richard Haass [president of the Council on Foreign Relations], for instance, who has long favored a change of strategy from "counterinsurgency" to "counterterrorism," now uses the budget crisis to bolster his case— although he leaves unclear how much money would be saved by such a shift in strategy. . . .

The Alleged Wars of Choice

Thanks to Haass's clever formulation, there has been a great deal of talk lately about "wars of choice" as opposed to "wars of necessity." Haass labels both the war in Iraq and the war in Afghanistan "wars of choice." Today, many ask whether the United States can simply avoid such allegedly optional interventions in the future, as well as the occupations and exercises in "nation-building" that often seem to follow.

Although the idea of eliminating "wars of choice" appears sensible, the historical record suggests it will not be as simple as many think. The problem is, almost every war or intervention the United States has engaged in throughout its history has been optional—and not just the Bosnias, Haitis, Somalias, or Vietnams, but the Korean War, the Spanish-American War, World War I, and even World War II (at least the war in Europe), not to mention the many armed interventions throughout Latin America and the Caribbean over the course of the past century, from Cuba in 1898 to Panama in 1989. A case can be made, and has been made by serious historians, that every one of these wars and interventions was avoidable and unnecessary. To note that our most recent wars have also been wars of choice, therefore, is not as useful as it seems.

In theory, the United States could refrain from intervening abroad. But, in practice, will it? Many assume today that the American public has had it with interventions, and Alice Rivlin certainly reflects a strong current of opinion when she says that "much of the public does not believe that we need to go in and take over other people's countries." That sentiment has often been heard after interventions, especially those with mixed or dubious results. It was heard after the four-year-long war in the Philippines, which cost 4,000 American lives and untold Filipino casualties. It was heard after Korea and after Vietnam. It was heard after Somalia. Yet the reality has been that after each intervention, the sentiment against foreign involvement has faded, and the United States has intervened again.

Depending on how one chooses to count, the United States has undertaken roughly 25 overseas interventions since 1898. . . .

Possible Future US Military Interventions

Today there are a number of obvious possible contingencies that might lead the United States to substantial interventions overseas, notwithstanding the preference of the public and its political leaders to avoid them. Few Americans want a war with Iran, for instance. But it is not implausible that a president—indeed, this president—might find himself in a situation where military conflict at some level is hard to avoid. The continued success of the international sanctions regime that the [Barack] Obama administration has so skillfully put into place, for instance, might eventually cause the Iranian government to lash out in some way—perhaps by attempting to close the Strait of Hormuz. Recall that Japan launched its attack on Pearl Harbor in no small part as a response to oil sanctions imposed by a [Franklin] Roosevelt administration that had not the slightest interest or intention of fighting a war against Japan but was merely expressing moral outrage at Japanese behavior on the Chinese mainland. Perhaps in an Iranian contingency, the military actions would stay limited. But perhaps, too, they would escalate. One could well imagine an American public, now so eager to avoid intervention, suddenly demanding that their president retaliate. Then there is the possibility that a military exchange between Israel and Iran, initiated by Israel, could drag the United States into conflict with Iran. Are such scenarios so farfetched that they can be ruled out by Pentagon planners?

Other possible contingencies include a war on the Korean Peninsula, where the United States is bound by treaty to come to the aid of its South Korean ally; and possible interventions in Yemen or Somalia, should those states fail even more than they already have and become even more fertile ground for al Qaeda and other terrorist groups. And what about those "humanitarian" interventions that are first on everyone's list to be avoided? Should another earthquake or some other natural or man-made catastrophe strike, say, Haiti and present the looming prospect of mass starvation and disease and political anarchy just a few hundred miles off U.S. shores, with the possibility of thousands if not hundreds of thousands of refugees, can anyone be confident that an American president will not feel compelled to send an intervention force to help?

The Need to Maintain a Strong Military

Some may hope that a smaller U.S. military, compelled by the necessity of budget constraints, would prevent a president from intervening. More likely, however, it would simply prevent a president from intervening effectively. This, after all, was the experience of the [George W.] Bush administration in Iraq and Afghanistan. Both because of constraints and as a conscious strategic choice, the Bush administration sent too few troops to both countries. The results were lengthy, unsuccessful conflicts, burgeoning counterinsurgencies, and loss of confidence in American will and capacity, as well as large annual expenditures. Would it not have been better, and also cheaper, to have sent larger numbers of forces initially to both places and brought about a more rapid conclusion to the fighting? The point is, it may prove cheaper in the long run to have larger forces that can fight wars quickly and conclusively, as [former Secretary of State] Colin Powell long ago suggested, than to have smaller forces that can't. Would a defense planner trying to anticipate future American actions be wise to base planned force structure on the assumption that the United States is out of the intervention business? Or would that be the kind of penny-wise, pound-foolish calculation that, in matters of national security, can prove so unfortunate?

The debates over whether and how the United States should respond to the world's strategic challenges will and should continue. Armed interventions overseas should be weighed carefully, as always, with an eye to whether the risk of inaction is greater than the risks of action. And as always, these judgments will be merely that: judgments, made with inadequate information and intelligence and no certainty about the outcomes. No foreign policy doctrine can avoid errors of omission and commission. But history has provided some lessons, and for the United States the lesson has been fairly clear: The world is better off, and the United States is better off, in the kind of international system that American power has built and defended.

| *"If we were to restrain the global inter-*
ventionism . . . we could ensure our
safety while preserving our power."

US Military Power
Should Be Restrained and
Interventions Avoided

Harvey M. Sapolsky, Benjamin H. Friedman, Eugene Gholz, and Daryl G. Press

In the following viewpoint, Harvey M. Sapolsky, Benjamin H. Friedman, Eugene Gholz, and Daryl G. Press argue that the United States should stop acting as the world's police force. The authors call for a new strategy of restraint that involves rethinking alliances, focusing counterterrorism strategies on intelligence, and reducing the number of overseas interventions and military bases. Sapolsky is a professor of public policy and organization at the Massachusetts Institute of Technology (MIT). Friedman is a research fellow in defense and homeland security studies at the Cato Institute. Gholz is an associate professor of public affairs at the University of Texas at Austin, and Press is an associate professor of government at Dartmouth College.

Harvey M. Sapolsky, Benjamin H. Friedman, Eugene Gholz, and Daryl G. Press, "Restraining Order: For Strategic Modesty," *World Affairs*, Fall 2009.

As you read, consider the following questions:

1. The authors contend that foreign military operations by the United States have led to a neglect of what four domestic issues?

2. Declaring war on terrorists who do not target Americans causes what, according to the authors?

3. The authors claim that one obstacle to implementing a strategy of restraint is in overcoming what Cold War–era assumption?

Even in an era of globalization, when information, people, goods, services, and, yes, weapons, armies, and terrorists may travel much more efficiently than in the past, geography still matters. At the start of the Cold War, the United States chose to relinquish the protection given by wide ocean buffers and relatively unthreatening neighbors to protect poor and depleted European and Asian allies whose own geography made them vulnerable to Soviet expansion. Today, however, the Cold War is long over, these allies have grown prosperous, and it's time for America to reclaim its strategic depth.

A Different Grand Strategy

The Cold War left a legacy that has been difficult for Americans to transcend. The global network of American bases and military commands is ready for use, and many U.S. allies, despite their posturing complaints about U.S. policy, often encourage our interventionism as a way of ducking responsibility for maintaining their own security. It is also true that post–Cold War conflicts that developed in or near the collapsed Soviet empire, and the violent ethnic rivalries and failed states of Africa and Asia, have tempted U.S. intervention. When President [Barack] Obama and other policymakers claim that security is indivisible—that instability anywhere threatens American security and prosperity everywhere—they are saying that the United States must undertake the burden because someone has to do it.

The United States would be better off pursuing a different grand strategy, one that would regain the advantages of our geography and accustom our friends once again to carrying the responsibility for their own security. Though we are the globe's strongest nation—with a very powerful military, the world's largest economy, and an enticing culture—we have neither the need nor the resources to manage everyone else's security. We can meet the challenges of globalization and terrorism without being the self-appointed and self-financed global police force.

Restraint would offer the opportunity to reinvigorate the foundations of America's strength. Foreign distractions, among other causes, have led the United States to neglect its transportation infrastructure, its educational system, its finances, and its technology base. If we were to restrain the global interventionism that has become our second nature since the end of World War II, we could ensure our safety while preserving our power to deal more precisely with threats that may materialize in an uncertain future.

The Challenge of Staying Safe

The first virtue of a restraint strategy is that it husbands American power. It acknowledges both America's great strengths—a combination of human and physical resources unmatched in the world—and the limitations of our power, which is easily dissipated in wasteful attempts to manage global security.

No nation or ideology now menaces American security in the same ways or to the same degree that the Soviet Union and Communism did during the Cold War. Instead, a variety of ethnic, religious, and nationalistic conflicts oceans away from us now obsess our policymakers, even though those conflicts have little to no prospect of spreading our way. To be sure, radical Islamists have attacked Americans at home and abroad, and while these attackers should be hunted down, they do not pose an existential threat, only a difficult and distracting one. Killing or capturing the criminals who attack Americans makes sense; trying to fix the failed states they call home is hopeless and unnecessary. The United States is safer than ever. The challenge now is staying safe.

The U.S. military is supposed to stand between America and hostile nations, but its forward deployment actually puts our forces between others and their own enemies. Alliances once meant to hold a coalition together against a common foe now protect foreign nations from adversaries that in most cases have no direct dispute with the United States. Although our allies are capable of fending for themselves, the fact that they can take shelter under an American umbrella allows them to defer taking responsibility for their own security. The United States should now use tough love to get our allies off our security dole. We need to do less so others will do more.

Not a Policy of Pacifism or Isolationism

Restraint should not be confused with pacifism. Calling for America to come home is different today than it was during the Cold War, when there was a world to lose. Today it is not a call for capitulation or disarmament, though it does provide an opportunity for force reductions. The restraint strategy requires a powerful, full-spectrum, and deployable military that invests heavily in technology and uses realistic training to improve capabilities and deter challenges. Restraint demands a military with a global reach that is sparingly used.

Similarly, restraint is not isolationism. Isolation avoids economic and diplomatic engagement and eschews potential profits from the global economy and the enrichment that sharing ideas and cultures can offer. The United States would be foolish to decline these opportunities. Restraint does not mean retreating from history, but merely ending U.S. efforts to try to manage it. Restraint would rebalance global responsibilities among America and its allies, match our foreign objectives to our abilities, and put domestic needs first.

The Costs of Alliances

A strategy of restraint would treat alliances as a means, not an end. Alliances are a way of sharing the price of working toward strategic goals. . . .

Policymakers should consider both the opportunities and the costs of alliances. Alliances are like off-balance-sheet liabilities whose risks only show up as costs on the rare occasions when the alliances get involved in high-profile crises and conflicts. Under the current dispensation, we often extend guarantees to our allies without considering the huge payouts.

Alliances are costly for another reason. They cause us to spread our military assets around the world, giving potential enemies U.S. targets in their own backyards rather than forcing them to pay the price of attacking the United States by crossing the oceans that separate us from them.

Moreover, policymakers generally ignore the investments alliances require in a larger U.S. force structure. In the past, politicians have often explained that America's partners help pay the cost of basing the American military—a proposition that was always questionable but is certainly not true today as American forces shift to Eastern European, Middle Eastern, and Central Asian bases. American taxpayers often pay for basing rights rather than being paid for the military shield they provide our allies. (Even when Japan and Germany shared the burden of paying for Cold War bases, the United States paid full cost to train, equip, and develop the power-projection forces suited to America's established, long-term alliance commitments.)

Under a strategy of restraint, the United States would stop giving away American support. During the Cold War, inter-

ventionists could credibly argue that the vulnerability of allies was a direct threat to the United States, so we could not, for instance, afford to gamble that West Germany would resist Soviet blandishments if America's military shield was diminished or withdrawn altogether. Because everyone knew that we would ultimately come to the defense of a crucial ally, no matter how disloyal its diplomatic behavior or how small its defense investment, the United States was often hogtied in its alliances. Today, our own security is not so inseparably linked to that of our allies; the threats they face are less severe than in the Cold War, and they can afford to defend themselves. . . .

US Counterterrorism Policy

Three guidelines would shape U.S. counterterrorism policy under a strategy of restraint. The first is the importance of discernment, because we create enemies by too loosely defining who they are. The second is that a foreign policy that is less active in the Muslim world will diminish terrorism directed against Americans. The third is that counterterrorism should be mainly a policing and intelligence exercise. Military force has a role, but the over-militarization of counterterrorism wastes resources and likely will generate more problems than it solves.

The restraint strategy distinguishes terrorists who attack the United States from those who do not. We should work with states around the world to combat all terrorists—those who intentionally target noncombatants. The U.S. government should share information on suspected terrorists with other states, track their movements across borders, freeze their bank accounts, arrest them when they enter U.S. territory, and encourage other nations' counterterrorism efforts.

Terrorists who target America and its citizens are another matter. In pursuing them, a restraint strategy would employ all of the above policy tools while also pressuring countries to act against these organizations within their own borders. If a host country is unable or unwilling to hunt terrorists who attack America, the United States itself should act. That could include covert action directed at the terrorists, air strikes, small-scale raids, or in extreme circumstances an invasion.

The War on Terrorism

By contrast, declaring war on terrorists who do not target Americans invites obscure violent groups around the world to make us their enemies. A lack of discrimination in choosing whom to attack also strengthens terrorists by granting them recognition and encourages alliances between otherwise separate terror groups. Our enemy today, for instance, is not Islam, not Islamism, not Islamic fundamentalism, not Wahabism, not Salafists, and not even jihadists, per se. Our enemies are those who attack Americans and those who shelter them.

Most jihadists are fighting their local governments. In the long term, their struggle will probably fail. But their defeat will have to come at the hands of their compatriots, not from the liberal forces led by the United States. American participation in the political conflicts in the Islamic world makes the United States a target of the terrorists involved in those conflicts, and American involvement feeds the conspiracy theories that make supposed evildoers in Washington the excuse for all that goes wrong in the Middle East. Non-intervention in Middle Eastern politics should not be regarded as appeasement, but as a key component of counterterrorism.

In the rare circumstances in which the United States needs to invade or even occupy part of the Muslim world, as in Afghanistan, the U.S. military should diminish its footprint and limit its stay. The United States should not shrink from stating that we believe that liberal democracy is a good form of government, but we should model democracy rather than insisting that others adopt it. Though we should not be mute in the face of egregious human rights violations, Americans should stop telling people in the Muslim world how to run their countries. . . .

The Two Alternatives to Restraint

Each of the two main strategic alternatives to restraint, primacy and global engagement, suffers from major flaws. Primacists seek to contain peer-competitors to America, especially China. They hope to dissuade Beijing from building a military to match its growing economic power. Some even want to destabilize the Beijing government by accelerating China's liberalization in ways that would make modernization difficult to control, or by trying to embarrass the government (militarily or otherwise) in a way that would cause decades of political and economic disarray.

Such an anti-China strategy is unwise. First, it is far from guaranteed that China will continue its economic rise or successfully manage the social strains that its government already faces. And a policy of active containment (let alone a policy of destabilization) may even make it easy for leaders in Beijing to rally nationalist sentiment against the United States and distract attention from their own failings. This sort of anti-China strategy accomplishes only one thing for sure: it turns tomorrow's potential adversary into today's certain one.

A second strategic alternative to restraint is to continue America's muddled approach to international politics: global engagement, often mistakenly called "selective engagement." Advocates of this policy seek to protect the U.S. economy, as well as other overseas interests, by enhancing international law and order. In this telling, the United States is the sheriff, working with locals to keep the outlaws at bay while institutions for global governance take root.

This strategy vastly overstates America's ability to engineer the global system. We lack the expertise to manage distant corners of the world, and our efforts too often fan nationalist and tribal opposition. Ordering the world according to our liking involves picking winners and losers. The losers will blame us for their problems, the winners will resent our role in their success, and both sides will blame us when things go awry.

Global activism costs us in two other crucial ways. First, it forces us to violate our values when local stability requires tactical alliances with unsavory regimes. Second, it discourages our friends from becoming self-reliant, leaving us with weaker partners when we truly need them. Restraint better protects American interests.

Implementing a Strategy of Restraint

Implementing a strategy of restraint will be difficult because it requires us to overcome a belief that became ingrained in our worldview during the Cold War: the assumption that if we did not manage security affairs in every corner of the globe we would find ourselves on the defensive in a great ideological and military contest. Americans have learned to think it is our duty to fret over conditions in the Baltics, the Balkans, the Bosphorus, the Beqaa valley, the Persian Gulf, the Pashtun region, Thailand, Taiwan, and East Timor. Almost every country, no matter how small, distant, or unfamiliar, has been labeled "strategic" by some American official.

The second obstacle to overcome is our global military command structure. The geographically based commands reflexively lobby for involvement in their regions. Their plans drive our thinking about larger national security issues and impose unbounded demands on our resources. Regional commanders overshadow our diplomats and overburden our defense budget. The more Unified Combatant Commands the United States has, the longer the list of certified threats and the less flexible our ability to respond due to the earmarking of forces. Doing away with the regional commands will improve strategic planning and our ability to weigh challenges and allocate our limited resources.

Some U.S. overseas bases vital to ongoing operations may have to be retained. Continuing arrangements with a few other nations may be necessary for fleet access. But a network of forward bases gives us an incentive to meddle and advertises our willingness to defend our hosts. We have been gradually reducing our global military presence for two decades. It is time to complete the mission. A homecoming for American forces would be a clear statement of our intent to follow a new grand strategy.

Restraint would also allow reductions in defense spending and force structure and help us realign military spending. For instance, restraint reduces the likelihood that the United States will find itself conducting two simultaneous high-intensity ground wars. The balance in forces should shift accordingly, and ground forces would absorb more than a proportional share of cuts. The United States spends vastly more on defense than any other country, and despite the cuts will retain military dominance in air, ground, and naval combat.

Using Power Cautiously and Frugally

A defense strategy of restraint would allow us to again make use of the natural barriers that separate us from most sources of danger in the world. That strategy encourages our allies to defend themselves. It stops us from occupying foreign countries under the misguided perception that we can and ought to remake them. It diminishes the perception abroad that the United States has become a revolutionary power bent on remaking the world, and it demonstrates that we intend to spread liberal values by example rather than force. This strategy husbands our power rather than wasting it fighting conflicts that need not involve us.

An America that is not on call for every conflict that breaks out in every corner of the world will have the time and resources to address the financial and infrastructure issues that weaken our domestic health and international power. The burden of providing security for others long after the need disappeared has simply caused us to neglect too much at home. More watchful waiting and less international meddling will preserve our security and wealth. We need to reclaim our strategic depth and stop our friends from free riding on our military. It is, finally, time to come home.

| *"Failure in Afghanistan will affect America's stature in the world."*

Success in the Afghanistan War Is Necessary to Protect America's Reputation

Peter Brookes

In the following viewpoint, Peter Brookes argues that the US military cannot walk away from the war in Afghanistan until it has succeeded in defeating the Taliban. Brookes warns that failure to contain the Taliban in Afghanistan would have global consequences, allowing the rise of violent Islamist movements around the world and making dangerous conflict likely with Afghanistan's neighbors. Brookes argues that America's standing in the world is at stake, and anything less than success in Afghanistan would undermine American leadership in the world. Brookes is a senior fellow for national security affairs at the Heritage Foundation and an adjunct professor at the National Defense University.

As you read, consider the following questions:

1. According to the author, what is the Taliban?

Peter Brookes, "Why We Can't Walk Away," *Armed Forces Journal*, November 2009. Reproduced by permission.

2. The author worries that US failure in Afghanistan would have negative impacts on which two nearby countries that have a history of fighting with each other?

3. Brookes worries that US failure in Afghanistan would harm US negotiations over nuclear and ballistic missile programs with which two countries?

There is certainly a lot of hand-wringing, chin-rubbing and forceful exhaling going on these days over the increasingly challenging war in Afghanistan, where nearly 70,000 U.S. troops are duking it out with the Taliban, al-Qaida and war lords.

Now [November 2009] into the ninth year since U.S. forces entered Afghanistan, support for the protracted fight among the American public, including members of Congress, is slipping as the [President Barack] Obama administration wrestles with a strategy with its trademark on it.

On the surface, it is understandable: There has been little good news of late in spite of the blood, sweat and tears of our brave troops and others, including U.S. diplomats and civilians, who are often on the front lines, too.

War assessments range from "serious" to "dire" to "deteriorating." Some long-term supporters of the war are saying it is time for Uncle Sam to pull up his tent stakes and come home. Others agitate for the U.S. to reduce its footprint and opt instead for a strategy where American troops support Afghan indigenous forces with training, intelligence, logistics, air and special operations capabilities.

So while the Obama administration—and the American public—mull Afghanistan, it is important to remember, especially in the long shadow of the eighth anniversary of Sept. 11 [2001, terrorist attacks], that the stakes are still high for us in that seemingly remote South Asian nation.

The Threat of Taliban Takeover

Of course, we do not want to turn Afghanistan over to the Taliban, a repressive, Islamist terrorist group, which has surged in recent years from safe havens in the Pakistani tribal belt along the inhospitable border with Afghanistan. Indeed, after battling American and coalition (largely NATO [North Atlantic Treaty Organization]) forces for years, the current breed of Taliban fighter is reportedly even more anti-West than his predecessors were in the 1990s. This is not good news; they are serious about the fight.

The Taliban is set on having control over Afghanistan (again), which is a distinct possibility without appropriate opposition, according to recent assessments. Already making plans for such a takeover, the Taliban has killed more than 100 Afghan tribal leaders who might block their ascent to power in Kabul [capital of Afghanistan]. The creation of a fundamentalist "Talibanistan" would put the country in the hands of an acknowledged terrorist group, resulting in serious security repercussions for the region—and beyond. With the Taliban in charge in Afghanistan, al-Qaida would almost certainly have a free hand to return and set up camps similar—or larger—to what they had in the late 1990s in the run-up to Sept. 11 [2001], allowing them to recruit, plan and train for terrorist attacks abroad—including against the U.S.

With military pressure being applied on the Pakistani side of the border, al-Qaida would surely return to its old stomping grounds in large numbers, where it would almost certainly be able once again to strike a deal with its former landlords, the Taliban. And as some have suggested, even if al-Qaida were not invited back by the Taliban, could they keep its inspirational leader Osama bin Laden from returning if he wanted to, making Afghanistan a magnet for followers?

This means that failing to defeat the Taliban insurgency will have global consequences in that Afghanistan would become, once again, an al-Qaida safe haven from which it could freely propagandize, plot and operate, advancing its global jihad.

The Risk of Talibanization

Simply put: Al-Qaida in Afghanistan cannot be defeated without prevailing over the Taliban as well. Like a parasite in a symbiotic relationship, al-Qaida feeds off host Islamist insurgencies such as the Taliban's—and from them, gains strength. (Likewise, the Taliban benefits from its links to al-Qaida, including ideological inspiration and military and terrorist training.)

Losing to the Taliban in Afghanistan would also put wind in the sails of other violent Islamist movements across the planet, which would see hope in the defeat of the world's most powerful country by a relatively small group of insurgents. Indeed, like al-Qaida, some might also choose to make Afghanistan an operating base. For instance, the Taliban has long had ties with the Islamic Movement of Uzbekistan—or IMU—which fought alongside Mullah Omar's group during the Afghan civil war in the 1990s and is active in nearby Uzbekistan, Tajikistan and Kyrgyzstan.

With the fall of Kabul to the Taliban—and with the Taliban's assistance—we could very well see the creeping "Talibanization" of Central Asia and the strengthening of terrorist groups such as the IMU, undermining the already-threatened stability of that region.

Dealing a blow to the Taliban in Afghanistan, on the other hand, would have a salutary effect well beyond that country, increasing the security of those who find themselves in terrorist cross-hairs, whether in Europe or Asia.

The Link Between Afghanistan and Pakistan

But while the war in Afghanistan is often reduced to a fight on terror, it's about what happens next door in Pakistan, too.

Failing in Afghanistan could lead to (more) challenges in already-troubled neighboring Pakistan, where the Taliban—and other Islamist extremists—have the national government in Islamabad squarely in their sights. The Taliban wields significant influence in Pakistan along the vast Afghan-Pakistan border. Indeed, according to some experts, the Taliban is actually more popular in Pakistan than in Afghanistan, increasing the threat from the group. But while Islamabad has made gains in pushing the Taliban back, it was just last spring that the Taliban controlled the Swat Valley, coming within 60 miles of the nation's capitol. At the time, some predicted that the fall of the Islamabad government was in the offing. (There is a certain irony in that the Pakistan Inter-Services Intelligence [ISI] directorate supported the creation of the Taliban in the 1990s to protect Islamabad's interests in Afghanistan.)

Unfortunately, Taliban troubles continue to grow in such regions as Waziristan in the Federally Administered Tribal Areas as well as urban areas such as Quetta in the southwestern province of Baluchistan, from where analysts believe senior Afghan Taliban leaders are running their operations into southern Afghanistan. The last thing any security analyst wants to see is the Pakistan government fall to terrorists like the Taliban, which would unleash a Pandora's Box of problems for those with anti-terror and regional interests.

But, it is a distinct possibility, especially if Afghanistan goes bad.

Losing in Afghanistan to the Taliban—or even ceding a large swath of ground—could allow Afghan territory to become the reverse-image of Pakistan today, which the Taliban uses as a sanctuary for the cross-border assaults into Afghanistan. The inverse of this situation could quickly evolve, making Afghanistan the launching pad for the Taliban, al-Qaida or other Islamist groups to attack and topple the Pakistani central government. One outcome is that Pakistan, which is already home to a number of Islamist terrorist groups such as

Jaish-e-Mohammed and Lashkar-e-Taiba, could become even more of a hotbed for regional and extra-regional terrorism. Even worse, if the Taliban topples the Pakistan government, it is conceivable that an even bigger nightmare might come to pass: The terrorist Taliban comes into possession of Islamabad's arsenal of a few hundred nuclear weapons. What this would mean for the prospects of nuclear terrorism, proliferation or the use of these weapons between states is anyone's guess—and a good basis for insomnia.

In the end, Pakistan and Afghanistan are inextricably linked: Failure in one country will contribute to failure in the other—just as success in either Afghanistan or Pakistan will increase the likelihood of a positive result across the border.

Afghanistan's Other Neighbors

But it is not just Pakistan that has a lot at stake in Afghanistan. Neighboring India, the South Asian giant, is also nervous about Afghanistan's future, which is another area of competition—and proxy conflict—with rival Pakistan. The now-nuclear armed India and Pakistan have come to blows (and near-blows) a number of times since their independence from the British Empire in 1947. Not surprisingly New Delhi is worried about Islamabad having significant influence in neighboring Afghanistan. India, a markedly terrorism-afflicted state, also worries that Afghanistan could become an operating base for Islamist extremists under the control of Pakistan with the aim of seeking to influence policies regarding Muslim-dominated Kashmir, a long-contested area between Islamabad and Delhi. Indeed, most experts acknowledge that Pakistan views the Afghan Taliban as an asset, seeing them as an ace-in-the-hole to limit Indian influence in Afghanistan, especially if the western forces were to leave precipitously.

India and Pakistan, both powerhouses in their own rights, are not only important partners of the United States in fighting terrorism, but in dealing with a host of other key issues, such as nuclear non-proliferation and Iran. Positive relations between them are critical to American interests.

Iran is also quite interested in happenings in neighboring Afghanistan and has been supporting its former nemesis, the Taliban, and others with weapons, including IEDs [improvised explosive devices], used in fighting coalition forces. It is not clear what sort of relationship a post-conflict Taliban would have with the Iranians, since they have been sworn enemies in the past, but it is very likely Tehran would seek influence in Afghanistan to check unwelcome policies right next door.

American and coalition success in Afghanistan is important for containing Iranian influence in the region, which has been surging not only across the Middle East, but into neighboring regions such as Central Asia. We could also see big power competitors of the United States, namely Russia and China, move significantly—although not militarily—into the region to influence outcomes since Afghanistan is on their periphery and both have concerns about Islamist movements among their populations.

The Impact on America's Reputation

And, of course, failure in Afghanistan will affect America's stature in the world.

As the Afghan situation unfolds in the months to come, both friends and foes will be watching closely for even subtle signs of American intentions, especially its commitment to continuing the fight.

Not surprisingly, a lot of strategic hedging is going on among stakeholders in Afghanistan as America works out its strategy. Even a seeming lack of resolve will have consequences, as Afghanistan Commander Gen. Stanley McChrystal said recently in a speech in London: "Uncertainty disheartens our allies, emboldens our foe."

But it goes beyond that.

Perceptions of who is winning and who is losing and who is staying and who is going affect the civilian population in Afghanistan—one that is famous for bending with the prevailing political winds. Having the population on the right side is critical to any counterinsurgency campaign.

It is also not outlandish to assume that defeat in Afghanistan to the Taliban would leave the United States looking soft and undependable with both allies and enemies, having a negative effect on American interests across the globe.

For example, failure in Afghanistan will ripple into NATO, where America's leadership will be undermined, perhaps, convincing the Europeans of the soundness of their parallel effort to establish a European Union defense policy and force. Asian allies would certainly wonder about their American partner, too.

Moreover, coming up short in Afghanistan certainly would not encourage the likes of the recalcitrant regimes in Iran or North Korea to come around to our way of thinking on negotiations over their nuclear and ballistic missile programs.

And as the Pakistani foreign minister, Makhdoom Shah Mahmood Qureshi, plainly told the *Wall Street Journal* recently about a U.S. withdrawal before the Taliban is defeated: "This will be disastrous . . . you will lose credibility . . . who is going to trust you again?"

A Necessary War for Security

Beyond big power politics, and although seemingly counterintuitive, Afghanistan has proven via the horrors of 9/11 that in some cases it is the weakest nations—especially failed states—that can be the source of some of the most significant national security threats.

As Gen. Stanley McChrystal, perhaps less than eloquently, put it: Leaving Afghanistan before the job is done would create "Chaos-istan." That certainly would not be in anyone's interest, except maybe terrorists and criminals.

Obama was right to say this is a war of necessity, that the "safety of the people around the world is at stake" in Afghanistan, and that "If left unchecked, the Taliban insurgency will mean an even larger safe haven from which al-Qaida would plot to kill more Americans."

Among experts, this is not disputed.

The challenge now for the American national security establishment is to develop and resource the right strategy for succeeding in Afghanistan—because failure just does not present any attractive outcomes for U.S. interests.

| *"Failing to 'win' would be bad. But carrying on in a war not worth fighting would be worse."*

Continuing the War in Afghanistan Will Harm America's Reputation

Doug Bandow

In the following viewpoint, Doug Bandow argues that there are insufficient US interests to justify continuing to fight the war in Afghanistan. Bandow claims that the situation in Afghanistan is poor, despite years of US sacrifice in the country. Furthermore, he claims there is little hope for improvement because security forces in Afghanistan are inadequate and the Hamid Karzai government is corrupt. He contends that recent US military operations illustrate the hopelessness of US involvement in Afghanistan, and he concludes it is time for America to leave the country. Bandow is a senior fellow at the Cato Institute, specializing in foreign policy and civil liberties.

As you read, consider the following questions:

1. Bandow claims that Afghanistan was a relatively stable country prior to what year?

2. What percentage of the Afghan National Army (ANA) and Afghan National Police (ANP) are capable of independent action, according the Bandow?

3. According to the author, do most Americans believe the war in Afghanistan is worth fighting?

Republican National Committee Chairman Michael Steele recently said the unthinkable: Afghanistan is "a war of Obama's choosing." Steele's remarks triggered a verbal slugfest between neocon [neoconservative] proponents of endless war, such as William Kristol, and Iraq hawks turned Afghanistan doves, such as Ann Coulter.

Michael Steele was right. President Barack Obama could have started afresh in Afghanistan. But he chose to make the war his own, twice escalating the number of troops.

US Interests in Afghanistan

For what purpose? Baker Spring of the Heritage Foundation declared: to "defend the vital interests of the United States."

What vital interests?

The original justification for war long ago disappeared. Al-Qaeda has relocated to Pakistan. Today, says CIA [Central Intelligence Agency] Director Leon Panetta, "At most, we're looking at 50 to 100, maybe less" al-Qaeda operatives in Afghanistan.

Nevertheless, [former US ambassador to the United Nations] John Bolton argues that the Taliban and al-Qaeda must be defeated lest they "reconquer Afghanistan and make it a base for international terrorism." However, the Taliban leadership, which appeared unhappy that its guests brought the wrath of Washington down upon them back in 2001, likely would avoid a repeat performance.

In any case, al-Qaeda and other terrorists don't need Afghanistan to plan their operations. Pakistan's northwest has proved to be a hospitable home. Somalia and Yemen also offer sanctuaries. Other failed or semi-failed states could similarly host terrorists.

It's hard to fathom another reason for staying. Would withdrawal harm U.S. credibility? Perhaps. But a disappointing withdrawal is likely at some point. The longer Washington stays, the greater will be its loss of face.

The *Economist* magazine worries about "a civil war that might suck in the local powers, including Iran, Pakistan, India and Russia," which would eventually "end up harming America too: it always does." Yet whatever the U.S. does, these powers continue vying for influence, perhaps violently. Washington would be better off not involved.

Of course, leaving Afghanistan a better place is a worthy objective—the *Economist* even calls it "a duty" after having "invaded their country"—but is not easily achieved through outside military intervention. Civilian dead in Afghanistan may run 10,000. The majority of these deaths were caused by the Taliban, but as fighting grows more intense more civilians will be killed, injured, or maimed.

And Americans are directly responsible for many deaths. Gen. Stanley McChrystal complained in March [2010]: "We've shot an amazing number of people and killed a number and, to my knowledge, none has proven to have been a real threat to the force." Tens of thousands of Afghans have fled to Pakistan and up to 320,000 have been displaced within their own nation.

The Situation in Afghanistan

There are still Afghans who hope to create a liberal society. In fact, prior to the ouster of the king in 1973, Afghanistan was a relatively stable and peaceful land. Alas, that Afghanistan is gone. Like Humpty Dumpty, there's no way to put it back together again—at least, not in a reasonable amount of time at a reasonable cost.

Washington already has been at war in Afghanistan for nearly nine years. Yet after America's sacrifice of more than a thousand lives and expenditure of some $345 billion, the country remains a wreck. Gen. David Petraeus points to increased child immunizations and cell phone use, but those measures mean little in terms of Afghanistan's political future.

In June Gen. McChrystal, then commander of U.S. forces in Afghanistan, briefed NATO [North Atlantic Treaty Organization] members. He indicated that just five of 116 areas were rated "secure." In only five of 122 districts was the government assessed as exercising full authority.

Taliban attacks are up. The Afghanistan Rights Monitor recorded 1200 violent incidents in June, the highest monthly total since early 2002. The group complained that "the insurgency has become more resilient, multi-structured and deadly." When I visited in May [2010] allied personnel warned that many of the areas in which they operated have become much more dangerous. A NATO spokesman recently admitted: "I don't think anyone would say we're winning."

Still, John Nagl of the Center for a New American Security contends that the conflict is winnable "because for the first time the coalition fighting there has the right strategy and the resources to begin to implement it, because the Taliban are losing their sanctuaries in Pakistan and because the Afghan government and the security forces are growing in capability and numbers."

Yet there's less here than meets the eye. First, allied manpower remains inadequate. Traditional counter-insurgency doctrine suggests the necessity of deploying more than 600,000 troops, which would mean quintupling current force levels.

The answer won't come from Islamabad. John Bolton, for one, wishes Pakistan to take an active role in "the grim, relentless crushing of the Taliban and al-Qaeda." But the Pakistani military has no interest in participating in such a mission. Only at great cost has Islamabad managed to wrest some territory away from the Pakistani Taliban, and it has done so because these forces are seen as a threat to the Pakistani state.

Not so the Afghan Taliban, a tool of the Pakistani military for more than a decade. Islamabad has played a double game since America's intervention, aiding the Pashtun Taliban forces. Gen. McChrystal warned of Pakistan's failure "to curb insurgent support." One Westerner working with the Afghan government was even blunter, telling me: "Pakistan is in a state of undeclared war with NATO and Afghanistan. No one knows what to do."

Afghan Security Forces

Nor is salvation likely to come from an increasing number of Afghan security personnel. A recent report from the Office of the Special Inspector General for Afghanistan Reconstruction [SIGAR] noted that the U.S. had spent $27 billion so far on training the Afghan National Army (ANA) and Afghan National Police (ANP). Only 23 percent of the ANA and 12 percent of the ANP were rated in the top of four categories, meaning they were capable of independent action.

Even these numbers overstate the forces' capabilities. SIGAR cited "significant levels of regression, or backsliding, in the capability levels of fielded army and police units." Police instructors call them "illiterate, corrupt, and trigger-happy." On my recent trip one Afghan complained that sending in the ANP is the best way to turn people into Taliban.

The ANA has a better reputation, but the *Daily Telegraph* reported that "Many NATO troops have hair-raising stories of careless young Afghan soldiers accidentally firing their weapons, including rocket launchers," as well as of Afghan troops

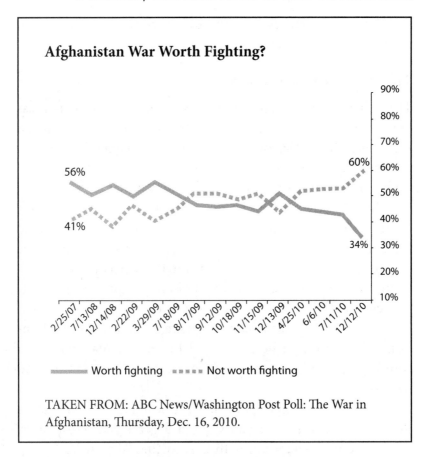

Afghanistan War Worth Fighting?

TAKEN FROM: ABC News/Washington Post Poll: The War in Afghanistan, Thursday, Dec. 16, 2010.

declaring that they are ending their patrol since it is lunchtime. Ironically, one of the Army's advantages is that it is deployed away from people, not among them, so its failings have less direct impact on the civilian population.

Then there is the Afghan government. Contrary to Vice President Joe Biden's claim, the U.S. is involved in nation-building. In the 2007 counter-insurgency manual, Gen. David Petraeus wrote: "Soldiers and Mariners are expected to be nation-builders as well as warriors." Moreover, "They must be prepared to help re-establish institutions and local security forces and assist in rebuilding infrastructure and basic services. They must be able to facilitate establishing local governance and the rule of law."

All of these require a viable Afghan government. However, such a government does not exist.

The Afghan Government

The Taliban is not particularly popular. Rather, in many areas the government is less popular. Tom Ricks of the *Washington Post* notes: "Our biggest single problem in Afghanistan is not the Taliban. They are a consequence of our problem. Our problem in Afghanistan is the Kabul government."

The [President Hamid] Karzai regime is noted more for corruption than competence. The *Los Angeles Times* [David Zucchino] writes of "a cabal of Afghan hustlers who have milked connections to high government officials to earn illicit fortunes." They have turned Afghanistan's capital into a vampire city, in which the elite live off of drug or Western money. I asked a long-time associate of President Karzai about allegations of corruption; he responded that no Afghan politician could long survive without "taking care of" his family and friends.

The Afghanistan Rights Monitor worries: "It will take a miracle to win the war against the insurgents and restore a viable peace in Afghanistan with the existing Afghan leadership and government." The country "lacks the basic prerequisites for a sustainable peace—a legitimate, competent and independent government and leadership."

Operations in Marja and Kandahar

The daunting challenge facing the U.S. is evident from operations in both Marja and Kandahar. The town of Marja was a Taliban sanctuary targeted by the U.S. military in February. The *Washington Post* [Rajiv Chandrasekaran] reported in June: "Firefights between insurgents and security forces occur daily, resulting in more Marine fatalities and casualties over the past month than in the first month of the operation." In May Gen. McChrystal complained of the perception that Marja had become "a bleeding ulcer." There simply is no "government-in-a-box" for Kabul to deliver as planned.

Even super-hawks Frederick and Kimberly Kagan acknowledge that Marja was "an area that supported insurgents precisely because it saw the central government as threatening and predatory." The allied operation has gone poorly because of "The incapacity of the Afghan government to deliver either justice or basic services to its people." The Kagans argue that U.S. forces have achieved more important military objectives. But those goals ultimately remain secondary to political progress.

There seems little reason to be optimistic about the chances of the far larger operation planned for Kandahar. The military campaign has been put off from June and support for the Taliban remains worrisomely strong. Moreover, the insurgents have been carrying out a campaign of assassination against Afghans friendly to the allies.

Again, success will depend on effective local governance. Yet *Los Angeles Times* reporter David Zucchino writes: "Development projects have been modest and plagued by insurgent attacks or threats against Afghan workers. Residents complain of shakedowns by Afghan police. Many U.S. troops say they don't fully trust their nominal allies in the Afghan police or army, who are scheduled to take responsibility for security by next summer." Brutal, corrupt, and inefficient government rule is worse than brutal, less corrupt, and less inefficient Taliban control for many Afghans. "If anybody thinks Kandahar will be solved this year," one top military officer told the *New York Times*, "they are kidding themselves."

A Decline in Public Support

President Obama appears ready to abandon his promise to begin troop withdrawals next July, but time is not on his side. A poll in May found that 52 percent of Americans did not believe the war was worth fighting. With the Europeans also looking for the exits, Secretary of Defense Robert Gates declared at the June [2010] NATO summit: "All of us, for our publics, are going to have to show by the end of the year that our strategy is on the track, making some headway."

Last December President Obama told West Point cadets "As your commander in chief, I owe you a mission that is clearly defined and worthy of your service." Alas, Washington is pursuing the wrong objective in the wrong place. America's critical interests are to prevent Afghanistan from again becoming an al-Qaeda training ground and avoid destabilizing next-door nuclear-armed Pakistan.

The first has been achieved, and could be maintained through a negotiated withdrawal with the Taliban—which likely would prefer not to be deposed again—backed by air/drone strikes and Special Forces intervention if necessary. The second would be best served by deescalating the conflict, which is a major source of instability in Pakistan.

Failing to "win" would be bad. But carrying on in a war not worth fighting would be worse. As Tony Blankley observes: "What is not inevitable is the number of American (and allied) troops who must die before failure becomes inevitable."

The Obama administration should focus on protecting Americans from terrorism. It should leave nation-building in Afghanistan to the Afghan people.

"The consequences of the link between democracy and American power are profound."

The United States Should Promote Democracy to Remain Powerful

John M. Owen IV

In the following viewpoint, John M. Owen IV argues that the promotion of democracy worldwide is in America's national interest and has positive effects for the whole world. Owen claims it is unsurprising that not all democracies support US promotion of democracy because such promotion tends to enhance the unipolarity of the United States—the primacy of US power. Even though democracy promotion can alienate others, Owen concludes that it is in the interest of the United States to pursue democracy promotion as a foreign policy goal. Owen is associate professor of politics at the University of Virginia and author of The Clash of Ideas in World Politics: Transnational Networks, States, and Regime Change 1510–2010.

John M. Owen IV, "Democracy, Realistically," *National Interest*, Spring 2006, pp. 35–42.

As you read, consider the following questions:

1. Owen claims that democracy promotion has been an official policy of the United States since when?

2. The author contends that the only country in the world that could be said to be trying to counter-balance US power is which nation?

3. The author gives what example of how US military intervention in Iraq has benefitted democracy?

Is America's national interest served by the spread of democracy? Realist critics have repeatedly chastised the [George W.] Bush Administration for its "utopianism", arguing that, in using American power to spread political liberty around the world, the president is at best wasting America's resources and at worst wooing disaster. These sentiments were clearly on display in the essay by Robert Tucker and David Hendrickson in the Fall 2005 issue of *The National Interest* and in the symposium that followed in the Winter issue. Many of the critics subscribe to the proposition that the promotion of democracy and the preservation of American power are contradictory goals; that the choice is either to embrace principle by promoting democracy (and paying a huge cost as a result) or to follow a self-interested policy and let other countries work out their domestic affairs with no guidance or interference from the United States.

The Link Between Democracy and American Power

In contrast, those who define themselves as "principled realists" (or "pragmatic idealists") believe that there is a close connection between the growth of American power and the spread of democracy. The United States reaps what economists term "efficiency gains" from the extension of democratic capitalism around the globe. Democracies conduct their affairs with a greater degree of transparency and reliability, making them more predictable partners for the United States. Because settled democracies do not fight wars against one another, America ends up with fewer enemies. As countries open up their economies, the United States gains more trading and investment partners. New democracies—particularly those in unstable regions of the world or those who find themselves located near powerful authoritarian neighbors—tend to forge much closer links with the United States.

The expansion of the zone of democracies since the 1980s is due in part to America's victory in the Cold War. The same expansion has in turn helped sustain American hegemony in the post-Cold War world. The consequences of the link between democracy and American power are profound. Realists must realize that preserving American power requires some democracy promotion. A democratic crusade—using force to bring liberty and justice to all without regard to cost—is never prudent, and indeed democracy promotion alone is insufficient grounds for a war. But the spread of free institutions has a rightful place among U.S. foreign policy goals, not least because it can serve the pre-eminent goals of national security and prosperity. This is why the United States has declared democracy promotion to be official policy since June 1982, when President Ronald Reagan announced to the British House of Commons, "The objective I propose is quite simple to state: to foster the infrastructure of democracy, the system of a free press, unions, political parties, universities, which allows a people to choose their own way to develop their own culture, to reconcile their own differences through peaceful means."

Critics of Democracy Promotion

Critics of democracy promotion are correct that, as Hamas's recent victory [January 2006] in Palestinian elections shows, abrupt free elections in authoritarian societies may produce anti-American governments. But stable democracy consists of institutions and culture, not simply an election certified by [former President] Jimmy Carter. And it is true that some advocates of vigorous American democracy promotion fail to appreciate that some countries lack so many prerequisites for liberal democracy that even the world's sole superpower cannot democratize them at acceptable cost. Indeed, although sometimes democracy can be promoted by force of arms, in most cases such methods appear imperialistic and lead potential democrats in the target country to resist the promoter. But critics of democracy promotion go too far when they imply an inescapable trade-off between doing good—promoting liberty—and doing well—safeguarding U.S. interests. Sometimes good things do go together.

Yet the link between democracy and American interest implies another dynamic that all sides of the debate must come to grips with. States anxious to limit or roll back American power and influence in the world understand this link. Not surprisingly, these countries are not helping the United States promote democracy in Iraq. Indeed, their number includes some of America's fellow democracies, who have been put in the awkward position of opposing the overthrow of dictatorial regimes they abhor. Stable, secure democracies do not need U.S. help and are less pro-American than new democracies whose regimes are more threatened internally or externally. Precisely because more democracies mean more American power and influence, democracy promotion will often be a unilateral U.S. action.

The Positive Impact of Democracy

Overall, the expansion of democracy over the past three decades has been a net gain not only for the United States but also for the world as a whole.

The near absence of wars among mature liberal democracies—perhaps the most robust finding in international relations research today—means that democratic states need not prepare for war against one another. This allows them to invest resources elsewhere that might have been used on such preparations.

Democracies reap other efficiency gains as well. They are evidently more likely to trade with and invest in one another, which tends to raise their rates of productivity growth. More generally, their institutions make them relatively transparent and constrained, which in turn allows them to reach more efficient bargains with one another, with less hedging than afflicts relations among non-democracies. Thus they are more likely voluntarily to join and abide by international agreements than other types of states, and to form and maintain effective regional organizations that pool power. The most successful international organizations tend to be the ones that comprise liberal democracies: the EU [European Union], NATO [North Atlantic Treaty Organization], the OSCE [Organization for Security and Co-operation in Europe] and the OECD [Organisation for Economic Co-operation and Development].

Taken together, these advantages mean that, broadly speaking, the more democracies there are in the world, the better off is each democracy. Of course, as Adrian Karatnycky argued in these [*National Interest*] pages in [Summer] 2004, the fact that democracies form a sort of club, and a powerful and successful one at that, threatens authoritarian states to some degree. The non-democracies may respond by increasing their own military spending, forming alliances or otherwise threatening the democracies, and hence driving back up the costs of being democratic. But the expansion of the zone of democracy lessens the overall potential of non-democracies to harm democracies. Moreover, even an authoritarian state like China benefits, because the Chinese economy today depends so heavily on the prosperity of democracies (including the United States). Thus a "peace dividend" followed the collapse of the

Soviet empire, allowing U.S. military spending to decline by more than 20 percent from 1986 to 1994.

American Primacy in the Unipolar Era

So the United States gains each time a country becomes democratic. But there are tangible benefits beyond increases in economic well-being and decreases in security expenditures. The expansion of democracy over the past several decades has increased the number of American allies throughout the world. Most strikingly, the states of Central Europe, once freed from communism, quickly sought membership in NATO. Even democracies that do not seek a military alliance with the United States and that worry about unipolarity are unwilling to mount much of a challenge to it. Since most Latin American countries have embraced liberal democracy in recent decades, the United States has had few security concerns in that region (and, tellingly, it is only with left-authoritarian Cuba and Venezuela that U.S. relations are truly hostile). In Africa and Asia, U.S. relations with the democracies—including regional powers South Africa and India—remain cordial.

Ever since the decline and fall of the Soviet Union, traditional balance-of-power realism has anticipated the formation of an anti-American alliance that would end unipolarity. So far, the only state that is even arguably trying to counterbalance U.S. power is authoritarian China, whose ruling elites know that more democracy in China means less influence for them and more for the United States. American hegemony— the unipolar era—is extended in time by the extension in space of democracy. Democracy is not just a consequence of American primacy, it is also a cause of it. And leaders in China and around the world know it. . . .

That new democracies are pro-American might explain why non-democracies such as China and Russia oppose [President George W.] Bush's democracy promotion. But why do many democracies likewise oppose it? Why do so many even

Democracy Promotion and National Security

U.S. Democracy Promotion in the Middle East has suffered a series of crippling defeats. Despite occasionally paying lip service to the idea, few politicians on either the left or right appear committed to supporting democratic reform as a central component of American policy in the region. Who can really blame them, given that democracy promotion has become toxic to a public with little patience left for various "missions" abroad? But as the [Barack] Obama administration struggles to renew ties with the Muslim world, particularly in light of the June 2009 Cairo speech, it should resist the urge to abandon its predecessor's focus on promoting democracy in what remains the most undemocratic region in the world.

Promoting democratic reform, this time not just with rhetoric but with action, should be given higher priority in the current administration, even though early indications suggest the opposite may be happening. Despite all its bad press, democracy promotion remains, in the long run, the most effective way to undermine terrorism and political violence in the Middle East. This is not a very popular argument. Indeed, a key feature of the post-[George W.] Bush debate over democratization is an insistence on separating support for democracy from any explicit national security rationale. This, however, would be a mistake with troubling consequences for American foreign policy.

Shadi Hamid and Steven Brooke,
"Promoting Democracy to Stop Terror, Revisited,"
Policy Review, *February 1, 2010.*

now refuse to help the United States build democracy in Iraq, even though they, too, would be better off if that country did not plummet into civil war or theocracy? Why do countries that have for years berated America for its hypocrisy, for crowning itself the paladin of liberty with one hand while propping up assorted psychopaths and criminals with the other, not at least applaud the Bush Administration for withdrawing that other hand now? Do we not edge toward a contradiction in the argument here? U.S. power and influence do not appear to be coterminous with the zone of democracies. Even during the [Bill] Clinton years, France was complaining about American "hyperpower" and calling for a multipolar world.

Democrats' Attitudes Toward America

Across countries, some democrats are indeed more pro-American than others. The degree to which democrats favor policies that are in U.S. interests depends on the degree to which liberal democracy is endangered in their own country. In the late 1940s West European democrats lived in fear of communist takeovers via trade unions, the general demoralized state of their societies, and for all they knew a Soviet invasion. It was these Europeans who pushed for a permanent U.S. security guarantee on the Continent, amounting to an unprecedented expansion of American power. Today by contrast, democracy in Europe is secure, and European democrats neither need U.S. support nor see so many common interests with the United States. They do not fear that America will attack them, and, enjoying all of the efficiencies of life in the democratic club, they are not actively counter-balancing U.S. power. But with significant exceptions, including Great Britain, they are finding passive ways to limit U.S. power, such as remaining aloof from the struggle in Iraq.

In the Middle East, on the other hand, democrats are in a death struggle with Islamists of various stripes (as well as with secular authoritarians and monarchists). One of the most pro-American cohorts in the world, rivaling the devotees of [conservative talk-show hosts] Rush Limbaugh and Sean Hannity, may be the young educated urbanites of Iran. If Muslim democrats can come to trust the United States as European Christian Democrats did in the late 1940s, they will likewise see many common interests with America. If they come to govern their countries, their national policies will be friendlier to U.S. interests. Over the ensuing years, should Islamic democracies become more secure internally and externally, they will need U.S. support less, and, like European democracies before them, they will find that countervailing interests start to loom larger. They will tend to distance themselves from America and align with other countries according to power, culture, ethnicity, economics or geography. America's challenges in the Middle East at that point will begin to resemble its challenges in Europe and Latin America today. Islamic democracies will worry about gains in U.S. power, yet, living under the benefits of American liberal hegemony, will not be sufficiently motivated to counter-balance the United States actively. America's relations with these democracies will have their tensions, annoyances and humiliations; but who would not choose such relations over those that the United States has historically had with the region?

Democracy in Iraq

But are current conditions in Iraq—which has become for many the definitive test of Bush's democracy promotion strategy—conducive to stable, pro-American democracy? Is Iraq like Germany in the late 1940s and the Philippines in the late 1980s? Or is it more like Tajikistan or Saudi Arabia today, where the Bush Administration evidently fears that no viable democratic faction is willing and able to rule out cooperation with the Islamist enemy? . . .

Even for those who accept a link between democracy and U.S. influence, it is open to debate whether using force to democratize Iraq was the right policy. The administration ought to have seen that although the first half of regime change— toppling Saddam [Hussein]—was going to be easy, the second half—implanting democracy—was not. Scholars disagree on the prerequisites for constitutional democracy, but Iraq lacked any state institutions free of authoritarian taint; any national unity free of naked coercion; or any history of the rule of law. If Iraq disintegrates, becomes a Shi'a-dominated theocracy or settles into semi-democratic status, then American power will not be enhanced. Still, despair is not called for. It is good to recall that liberal democrats in the past have prematurely consigned certain cultures or regions—Catholic, Asian, Germanic—to permanent despotism. And for all its costs, the Iraqi intervention has had some benefits. For example, the various Iraqi elections in 2005 have encouraged dissenters in other Arab countries to believe that democracy is possible for them as well. As Farid Ghadriy reported recently in *Middle East Quarterly*: "The U.S.-led occupation of Iraq has been a watershed [for democratic reformers] within the Middle East. Reformists inside Syria are encouraged by the events that transpired in Iraq, even if some are loath to admit it."

The Risk of Alienation

If it is true that democracy extends U.S. influence, then still another objection arises: Is not the United States, by promoting democracy, liable to trigger hostility and counterbalancing? Are we not already seeing this in Iraq itself, where the U.S. occupation seems to amount to a subsidy for Al-Qaeda's recruitment program? And what about other states concerned at the intrusion of U.S. power in Central and Southwest Asia and North Africa? What will be the long-term reactions of Russia, China and India? America's moves into Southwest Asia have aided the formation and deepening of the Shanghai Cooperation Organization, a sort of authoritarian club comprising China, Russia, Kazakhstan, Kyrgyzstan, Tajikistan and Uzbekistan. If America is promoting democracy to augment its national security, is not its behavior eventually going to prove self-defeating? . . .

Today, Islamism, a transnational ideology whose force is by no means spent, is a serious enough threat to outweigh some alienation of other countries. But just how alienated others become is in part a function of the means and velocity with which America promotes democracy. At this point, with Iraq unstable, the region inflamed and much of the world persuaded that America is bent on a global empire, it is doubtless wiser for Washington to use economic and diplomatic means to press for democratic reform than to use force on unfriendly states such as Iran or Syria. The world can comfort itself with the knowledge that in the long term, as explained above, secure Muslim democracies should follow their European predecessors and distance themselves from the United States.

Since the Bush Administration decided to make Iraq the vein through which the Muslim world would receive its injection of liberty, democracy promoters have themselves gotten a healthful injection of realism. Freedom may indeed be for everyone, but at present not everyone wants what they take to be American- or Western-style freedom, and those who do want it do not necessarily trust the Americans to help them achieve it. But realists who persist in regarding any democracy promotion as a waste of resources at best and latter-day Jacobinism at worst need to recognize that competing ideas about political order polarize people and states and create opportunities for American (or anti-American) influence. Idealists must come to grips with the fact that, if they want a freer world, they must put up with American hegemony; realists, with the fact that if they want America to stay powerful and secure, they must put up with some democracy promotion.

| *"The price of defending our nation cannot be spending years . . . in a vain attempt to give people who despise us a way of life they don't want."*

The United States Should Not Promote Democracy in the Islamic World

Andrew C. McCarthy

In the following viewpoint, Andrew C. McCarthy argues that US military intervention in the Islamic world should not be used for the promotion of democracy. McCarthy claims that US democracy promotion did not work in Iraq and will not work in Afghanistan. He contends that those who favor the promotion of democracy fail to see that Islamism, not just radical Islamist factions, is fundamentally at odds with democracy. McCarthy concludes that we should focus on promoting democracy at home. McCarthy is a senior fellow at the National Review Institute and is the author of The Grand Jihad: How Islam and the Left Sabotage America.

As you read, consider the following questions:

1. McCarthy claims that what argument used to justify the surge of troops in Iraq has also been made about Afghanistan?

2. The author says that there are how many Muslims, adherents of the religion of Islam, in the world?

3. McCarthy argues that even if democracy could be established in Islamic countries, America would not be safe from terrorists for what reason?

Right after 9/11 [2001], Pres. George W. Bush made a succinct demand of the Taliban: Hand over Osama bin Laden [leader of terrorist organization al-Qaeda] and his cohorts or face horrific consequences. The demand, the president emphasized, was non-negotiable. The Taliban refused, insisting that the U.S. produce evidence against al-Qaeda. Because Islamists—not just terrorists but all Islamists—believe the United States is the enemy of Islam, the Taliban also floated the possibility of rendering bin Laden to a third country. No deal, Bush replied. As promised, the consequences were swift and severe. Yet, two weeks into the first bombing raids, the president offered the Taliban a "second chance." [Taliban leader] Mullah Omar declined to take it. The invasion proceeded and the rest is history.

A Suggestion About Afghanistan

It's now a long, confused history. The distance we've traveled from the clarity of the first days is manifest in the Right's ongoing intramural skirmish over the eminent [conservative columnist] George Will's latest column.

Will has called for a steep reduction of our 60,000-strong military force (out of a total of about 100,000 coalition troops) in Afghanistan. That country, he argues, is an incorrigible mess where we're engaged more in social work than in combat. Instead, Will would have our forces retreat to offshore bases from which, "using intelligence, drones, cruise missiles, airstrikes and small, potent special forces units," American efforts could be concentrated on Afghanistan's "porous 1,500-mile border with Pakistan, a nation that actually matters." This suggestion comes just as other conservatives are backing a Pentagon proposal to add about 40,000 troops. They seek a counterinsurgency surge for Afghanistan, similar to the one they claim worked so well in Iraq three years ago.

The Comparison Between Iraq and Afghanistan

There's no question that the surge in Iraq resulted in the rout of al-Qaeda. For that reason, it has to be counted as a net success. It would have been a strategic disaster to retreat while al-Qaeda was present and fortifying itself.

But then there was the rest of the surge rationale: the claim that we needed to secure the Iraqi population so a stable government, one that would be a reliable ally against terror, could emerge. The same argument now is being made about Afghanistan. Have you taken a look at Iraq lately? We went there to topple Saddam [Hussein]; we stayed to build an Islamic "democracy," and the result is an Iranian satellite. The new Iraq is a sharia [Islamic religious law] state that wants us gone, has denied us basing rights for future military operations, has pressured a weak American president into releasing Iran-backed terrorists, has rolled out the red carpet for [Muslim militant group] Hezbollah, allows Iranian spies to operate freely (causing the recent ouster of the intelligence minister, who was an American ally), tolerates the persecution of religious minorities, and whose soon-to-take-power ruling coalition vows "not to establish relations with the Zionist entity"—a vow that would simply continue longstanding Iraqi policy, as Diana West points out. If that's success, what does failure look like?

Democracy-project naysayers (I've long been one) reluctantly supported the surge in Iraq because our nation could not allow al-Qaeda a victory there. By contrast, as [conservative columnist] Rich Lowry mentions in passing at The Corner, "al-Qaeda is not in Afghanistan." Rich's observation came in the course of chiding Will's advocacy of "counterterrorist strikes from a distance." But if al-Qaeda is not in Afghanistan, why do we still need 60,000 troops there, let alone 40,000 more? We don't invade other hostile countries where al-Qaeda is actually present (see, e.g., Iran, Kenya, Yemen, Somalia), and the likelihood of al-Qaeda's return is not enough to keep us in other countries where we're not wanted (e.g., Iraq). That is, we're already banking on our capacity to conduct counterterrorist strikes from a distance.

Saving Afghanistan from the Taliban

The reason for going to war in Afghanistan was that al-Qaeda was there. The Bush administration was content to live with the Taliban ruling Afghanistan. They are a tyrannical lot, but Islam doctrinally and culturally lends itself to tyranny. The Taliban's brutalization of the Afghan people was not our military concern. That was a problem for the State Department to take up with our "allies"—like Pakistan, which created the Taliban, and Saudi Arabia, which helped Pakistan sustain it. Our military issue with the Taliban was bin Laden. Had the Taliban agreed to our terms, there would have been no invasion of Afghanistan.

Notwithstanding al-Qaeda's departure, the idea now seems to be that we should substantially escalate our military involvement in Afghanistan to replicate the experiment that supposedly worked so well in Iraq. It's the age of [President Barack] Obama, so our commanders are talking not about combat but about a stimulus package to fight the "culture of poverty." As military officials described it to the *New York Times*, "the overriding goal of American and NATO [North

Atlantic Treaty Organization] forces would not be so much to kill Taliban insurgents as to make ordinary Afghans feel secure, and thus isolate the insurgents. That means using force less and focusing on economic development and good governance." This is consistent with the delusional belief that terrorism is caused by poverty, corruption, resentment, Guantanamo Bay, enhanced interrogation tactics, Israel—in short, anything other than an ideology rooted in Islamic scripture. But before we all laugh George Will out of the room, we might remember that the Taliban was not our reason for invading. We would not have gone to war to save Afghanistan from the Taliban—which is to say, to save Afghanistan from itself. . . .

A Failure to Identify the Enemy

There has been a fascinating point of alignment since 9/11 between the anti-war Left and the democracy hawks. Both sides have failed to identify the enemy: Islamists. The hard Left resists because it doesn't see Islamism as an enemy at all. The Islamists, like the Left, regard the United States as the problem in the world.

Democracy hawks are another matter. Their boundless faith in democracy blinds them to the severity of the Islamist challenge. For them, dwelling on Islam is counterproductive: If Islam is understood as a huge liability, Americans will rebel against the prohibitive costs, in lives and money, of democracy-building. So the democracy-hawk approach is either not to mention Islam at all or to absurdly portray it as a "moderating" influence that will help build stable democracies. They shame doubters into silence by decrying "Islamophobia" and "cultural condescension"—mortal sins these days. On some level, the democracy hawks may grasp that the threat here involves more than terrorism. But they've convinced themselves that if we could just get rid of the terrorists, the rest of the Muslims who abhor us would be brought around by democracy's light.

It's a fantasy, and we're betting our lives on it. So let me try to spell out the folly of the democracy project's fundamental assumptions.

Islamism and Terrorism

We like to think Islamism represents only a fringe of the world's 1.4 billion Muslims. But that's because we confound Islamists and terrorists. The terrorists—those who commit and materially support violent attacks—are a fringe (bigger than we'd like to think, but still a tiny minority). By contrast, Islamists may be a majority, and, if they're not, they constitute a very substantial minority.

Islamism is not terrorism. To be sure, Islamism includes terrorism in its arsenal. Still, there is major disagreement among Islamists about when violence should be used and how effective it is. In any event, we must fight the tendency to meld these concepts. Terrorism is a tactic that divides Muslims. Islamism is a belief system that unites tens of millions of Muslims. Abdurrahman Wahid, the former president of Indonesia, estimates what he calls the "radicalized" portion of the umma [Muslim World] at about 15 percent. I think he's low-balling it, but even if he's right, that would be about 200 million people.

So what is Islamism? It is the belief that Islam is not merely a religious creed but a comprehensive guide to human existence, conformity to which is obligatory, that governs all matters political, social, cultural, and religious, from cradle to grave (and, of course, beyond). The neologism "Islamist" was minted over three-quarters of a century ago by Hassan al-Banna, the founder of the Muslim Brotherhood. To this day, the credo of the Brotherhood is "Allah is our objective. The Prophet is our leader. The Koran is our law. Jihad is our way.

Dying in the way of Allah is our highest hope." The Brotherhood claims, preposterously, to have renounced terrorism. It maintains, more credibly, that it *is* the Muslim Nation, as in a mass movement representing what Muslims, broadly, believe.

Islamic Law and Jihad

The Brotherhood's Islam is called Salafism. Developed in the 19th century, Salafism calls for a return to the unalloyed Islam of the 7th-century founders. It is to be "unalloyed" in the sense that it should be stripped of modernizing influences— particularly Western influences. This is to be achieved by implementing sharia, the divine law designed to govern all aspects of life.

Implementing sharia is the aim of jihad. Because our government does not want to be seen as Islamophobic, we are discouraged from noting the palpable nexus between Islamic scripture and Islamist terror. Thus we're conditioned to think of jihad, a creature of Islamic scripture, as a form of madness—as if terrorists blew up buildings for no better reason than to blow up buildings. But jihad is a central tenet of Islam. It is the obligation to struggle in the path of Allah—to impose God's law everywhere on earth. Jihad can be savage, but it is not irrational.

Jihad is correctly understood as a military duty, but it need not be violent. That does not mean, as Islam's Western apologists claim, that jihad is some wishy-washy internal struggle to become a better person. To the contrary, just as war is politics by other means, violent force is one of several jihadist tactics by which the Muslim Nation seeks to install sharia. If non-Muslims are willing to accommodate sharia in their political, legal, and financial systems, combat is not required. Surrenders are happily accepted.

But jihad undeniably includes the duty to drive infidel armies out of Muslim countries by force—even infidels who see themselves as benign, progressive, good Samaritans rather than occupiers. In 2004, Sheikh Yusuf Qaradawi, the "nonviolent" Muslim Brotherhood's spiritual guide, issued a fatwa [religious ruling] calling on Muslims to fight the Americans in Iraq. He was zealously supported by the faculty at al-Azhar University in Cairo, the most authoritative voice of Islamic jurisprudence in the Arab world. A few months later, Alberto Fernandez, then the State Department's top spokesman in the region, gushed that Qaradawi was an "intelligent and thoughtful voice from the region . . . an important figure that deserves our attention." It was an idiotic thing to say, but it was said in recognition of the grim reality that Qaradawi is not a fringe figure. His influence is vast. Understand this: It is not just terrorists but millions of Muslims who believe Americans in Iraq and Afghanistan should be killed even if they believe they are risking their lives so that Muslims can have a better life.

Islamism and Western Democracy

Why should Islamism matter to us? Because, besides being the ideology that catalyzes jihadist terrorism and threatens our freedoms in sundry other ways, Islamism rejects the premises of Western democracy. Islamists believe that sharia is the perfect, non-negotiable blueprint for law and life, prescribed by Allah Himself. Therefore, Islamists reject the notion of free people at liberty to govern themselves, to legislate in contradiction to God's law. They reject freedom of conscience: Islam must be the state religion, and apostasy from Islam is a capital crime. They deny the principle of equality under the law between men and women, and between Muslims and non-Muslims. They abjure any semblance of Western sexual liberty: gay sex, adultery, and fornication are brutally punished. They countenance slavery. They encourage polygamy. I could go on, but you get the idea.

This is all horrifying to us, but that is because we are a different civilization. [Former Prime Minister of Great Britain] Tony Blair was wrong, as Will has realized in more recent times. Individual liberty and democracy are not "universal values of the human spirit." And our democracy-building enthusiasts are wrong, and unintentionally insulting to Muslims, when they intimate that the Islamic world will fall in love with our values once they taste a little freedom.

President Bush decried the "cultural condescension" of us democracy doubters. But the shoe of arrogance is on the other foot. Those of us who've studied Islam have never doubted its "aptitude for democracy" (to borrow Will's phrase). The issue has never been one of aptitude; it is about principled beliefs. Fundamentalist strains of Islam, including Salafism, have been developed by extraordinary minds. It is not that these Muslims fail to comprehend our principles; they reject them. They have an entirely different conception of the good life. They believe freedom is not individual liberty but individual submission to Allah's law. Their very conception of freedom is the opposite of ours. When we talk to them about "freedom," we are ships passing in the night.

That doesn't make the Islamists backward. They are convinced that Western liberalism and the Judeo-Christian veneration of reason in faith are corrupting influences that rationalize deviations from Allah's law and His natural order. They believe, instead, in a pre-ordered, totalitarian system in which the individual surrenders his freedom for the good of the umma—and in which sowing discord (i.e., engaging in what we think of as free speech) is a grave sin, on the order of apostasy [renunciation of religion]. They are wrong in this. Our civilization is superior to theirs, which is why we have flourished and they have faltered. But being wrong doesn't make them crazy. They don't want what we're selling, and they have their reasons.

Muslim Support for Islamism

Most of our uninformed national conversation about Islam since 9/11 has been about the degree of Muslim support for terrorism. If you're going to embark on a quest to remake the Middle East, that's the wrong question. We should be asking: What is the degree of Muslim support for Islamism? The answer to that question is: immense.

Islamism is the official creed of Saudi Arabia, which, as noted above, is risibly portrayed as a U.S. ally against terrorism. The Saudis have lavishly supported and collaborated with the Muslim Brotherhood since the 1950s, enabling the Brothers to spread Islamism globally, including in America and Europe. Islamism, moreover, is the dominant ideology in the Arab world and in much of Pakistan, Iran, and Afghanistan. It is strengthening in northern and eastern Africa. Despite decades of suppression, it is resurgent in Turkey. Even in Indonesia, where Islamism is not preponderant, it is a growing force.

The fact that Islamists disagree with their terrorist factions on tactics obscures the reality that they heartily agree with the terrorists' contempt for the West. Most of the places that are sources of Islamist terror do not want Western democracy. They want sharia.

The Failure of Democracy Promotion

We can't change that about them, and it cheapens us when we try. The State Department's new "democratic" constitutions for Afghanistan and Iraq are a disgrace: establishing Islam as the state religion and elevating sharia as fundamental law. That is not exporting our values; it is appeasing Islamism. It is putting on display our lack of will to fight for our principles, which only emboldens our enemies. Recall, for example, the spectacle of the Christian prosecuted for apostasy a couple of years back by the post-Taliban, U.S.-backed Afghan government. He had to be whisked out of the country because it's not safe for an ex-Muslim religious convert in the new Afghanistan. It's not safe for non-Muslims, period. We're not building a democratic culture.

Further, even if we could clear the hurdle that Islamists don't want Western democracy, there remains the problem that a Muslim country's becoming a democracy would not make us safer from Islamist terrorists. It is illogical and counter-historical to suppose otherwise. The 9/11 attacks were extensively planned, over long periods of time, in, among other places, Berlin [Germany], Madrid [Spain], San Diego [California], Florida, Oklahoma, and Connecticut. Clearly, thriving democracy in those places provided no security. The doctrine that democracy is preferable because democracies don't make war on one another applies only if your threat matrix consists of hostile nation-states. A transnational terror network with no territory to defend and no normal economic system lacks the incentives a democracy has to avoid war. And, far from discouraging terrorists, democratic liberties work to their advantage.

Focusing on Democracy at Home

We can't stop Muslim countries from being Islamist. That is their choice. It should be no concern of ours who rules them as long as they do not threaten American interests. When they inevitably do threaten us, or allow their territories to be launch pads for terrorists, we should smash them. But the price of defending our nation cannot be spending years—at a cost of precious lives and hundreds of billions of dollars—in a vain attempt to give people who despise us a way of life they don't want.

Meanwhile, we must accept that Islamism is our enemy and has targeted our constitutional system for destruction by slow strangulation via sharia. Instead of worrying about democracy in Afghanistan, we need to worry about democracy in America. The surge we need is at home: to roll back Islamism's infiltration of our schools, our financial system, our law, and our government. In addition to not being universal, the "values of the human spirit" are not immortal. If we don't defend them in the West, they will die.

Periodical and Internet Sources Bibliography

The following articles have been selected to supplement the diverse views presented in this chapter.

Doug Bandow	"From Good War to Bad Social Engineering," *Chronicles*, March 2010.
John Bolton	"We Must Crush the Taliban and Al Qaeda in a 'Long War' in Afghanistan," *Los Angeles Times*, July 1, 2010.
Leon T. Hadar	"The Moral Hazard of U.S. Global Interventions," *Huffington Post*, December 18, 2009. www.huffingtonpost.com.
Shadi Hamid and Steven Brooke	"Promoting Democracy to Stop Terror, Revisited," *Policy Review*, February 1, 2010.
Chalmers Johnson	"America's Unwelcome Advances: The Pentagon's Foreign Overtures Are Running into a World of Public Opposition," *Mother Jones*, August 22, 2008.
Robert Kagan	"The Need for Power," *Wall Street Journal*, January 20, 2010.
Paul R. Pillar	"Afghanistan Is Not Making Americans Safer," *Foreign Policy*, November 19, 2009. www.foreignpolicy.com.
Jim Talent	"A Constitutional Basis for Defense," Heritage Foundation, June 1, 2010. www.heritage.org.
Stephen M. Walt	"Why They Hate Us (I): On Military Occupation," *Foreign Policy*, November 23, 2009. www.foreignpolicy.com.
Michael Yon	"The War in Afghanistan Is Winnable," *National Review*, October 19, 2009.

Are Current US Economic Policies a Good Use of America's Global Influence?

Chapter Preface

Foreign aid is a fundamental component of the US international affairs budget and is considered by many as a key component of US foreign policy. One of the main rationales for US foreign assistance is national security. The United States increased aid to foreign countries significantly after World War II in an attempt to decrease the communist influence of the Soviet Union during the Cold War. Following the end of the Cold War, the United States decreased foreign aid in the 1990s. However, after the terrorist attacks in the United States on September 11, 2001, foreign assistance increased once again. Foreign aid can take the form of direct military assistance in order to meet US national security objectives or economic assistance for humanitarian measures, such as reducing poverty and improving health care. Even humanitarian measures are perceived by many as having a national security purpose, because poverty is seen as one of the causes of political instability leading to the rise of terrorist organizations.

The US government gives more than $58 billion a year in foreign assistance; in 2010 this amounted to approximately 1.7 percent of the US budget. Of that amount, more than half is managed by the State Department and the US Agency for International Development (USAID). This aid is organized around seven foreign assistance categories: Peace and Security; Democracy, Human Rights, and Governance; Health; Education and Social Services; Economic Development; Environment; and Humanitarian Assistance. The top four recipients of foreign aid in 2010 were Israel, Afghanistan, Pakistan, and Egypt, receiving aid with the purpose of enhancing US security concerns in the Greater Middle East. Receiving much less per country, but in the top ten, are Kenya, Nigeria, South Africa, and Ethiopia, which all receive aid that is primarily aimed at health and other humanitarian initiatives.

US aid to the Middle East has been particularly controversial. Aid to Israel, which is used for military purposes, is perhaps the most controversial. But US foreign aid to Egypt has come under increased scrutiny since the political uprising in 2011. Since the Israel-Egypt peace accord in 1979, the two countries have been the top two recipients of US foreign aid if one excludes the wars in Iraq and Afghanistan. With approximately $1.5 billion given to Egypt in 2010 and a similar request for 2011, some commentators question the wisdom of giving aid to Egypt now that President Hosni Mubarek has stepped down. Tom Curry of MSNBC asks, "If the $68 billion in aid the US has sent to Egypt since 1948 is seen as an investment in political stability in the Middle East, has the investment benefited US interests, or is it failing or perhaps even backfiring?"[1] James Phillips of the Heritage Foundation advises, "Washington should make future aid to whatever government emerges from this crisis contingent on that government's respect for the freedom of Egypt's long-suffering citizens."[2]

The economic policies of the United States have a far-reaching global influence. The billions of dollars given each year in foreign aid are particularly controversial, especially the aid that is used as military assistance. As the United States considers future foreign assistance, the political uprisings in Egypt and elsewhere in the Middle East will surely prompt a closer consideration of aid to these countries.

1. Tom Curry, "What the United States Has at Stake in Egypt," MSNBC.com, January 28, 2011. http://www.msnbc.msn.com/id/41317259/ns/politics/.
2. James Phillips, "Bringing Freedom and Stability to Egypt," *Heritage Foundation Web Memo*, no. 3125, January 28, 2011. http://www.heritage.org/research/reports/2011/01/bringing-freedom-and-stability-to-egypt.

"Sanctions can be helpful to the extent that they drive up the economic, diplomatic, and political costs that the regime must pay to continue on its present nuclear path."

Economic Sanctions on Iran Are Effective and Should Be Increased

James Phillips

In the following viewpoint, James Phillips argues that continuation of Iran's nuclear program warrants increased US economic sanctions. Phillips contends that because Iran relies on oil revenues to fund its nuclear program, economic sanctions aimed at this industry could be effective at slowing Iran's acquisition of nuclear weapons. He claims the United States should work to penalize countries that invest in Iran's energy sector. He concludes that increased economic sanctions also could help support domestic opposition to Iran's regime. Phillips is a senior research fellow for Middle Eastern Affairs in the Douglas and Sarah Allison Center for Foreign Policy Studies at the Heritage Foundation.

James Phillips, "Refocus on Iran: More Sanctions Needed," *Heritage Foundation Web Memo*, no. 3154, February 14, 2011. www.heritage.org. Copyright © 2011 The Heritage Foundation. All rights reserved. Reproduced by permission.

As you read, consider the following questions:

1. According to Phillips, what action by the Iranian government in Istanbul showed it is not serious about diplomatic resolution of its nuclear issue?

2. According to the author, how much money did Iran earn from oil exports from January to November 2010?

3. Chinese oil companies have signed agreements to invest how much money into Iran's energy sector, according to Phillips?

Iran's hostile regime has been one of the chief beneficiaries of the political turmoil that has convulsed Egypt and Tunisia, which distracted the United States and other countries from the ongoing standoff over Iran's nuclear program. The dramatic events diverted international attention from [Iranian capital] Tehran's stubborn refusal to negotiate an acceptable resolution of the nuclear issue at the failed Istanbul talks last month [January 2011]. There is a distinct danger that Tehran will conclude that growing regional instability is tilting the balance of power in its favor and give it greater latitude to withstand international pressure to rein in its nuclear weapons program.

The [Barack] Obama Administration should vigilantly refocus international attention on Iran's nuclear defiance, support for terrorism, and human rights abuses and ratchet up pressure on Iran's radical regime.

Iran's Nuclear Program

Tehran demonstrated that it is not serious about a diplomatic resolution of the nuclear issue by rejecting negotiations with the U.S., four other permanent members of the U.N. [United Nations] Security Council, and Germany at the January 21–22 talks in Istanbul. Tehran refused to discuss "Iran's nuclear rights," including its expanding uranium enrichment program, despite four rounds of Security Council sanctions requiring Iran to comply with its nuclear safeguard obligations. Iran spurned Western efforts to revive a 2009 proposal for a nuclear fuel swap that would have traded some of Iran's growing stockpile of low-enriched uranium for fuel for its Tehran research reactor ostensibly needed to produce medical isotopes. Tehran also demanded that sanctions be lifted as a precondition for any future talks.

Rather than ease sanctions in a myopic effort to salvage vapid talks, the Obama Administration should redouble efforts to escalate international sanctions on Iran's recalcitrant regime. Although Iran's uranium enrichment program has suffered technical delays, including some caused by the mysterious Stuxnet computer virus, Washington must not grow complacent about the amount of time remaining to dissuade Tehran from continuing its nuclear efforts.

Iran is estimated to already possess enough low-enriched uranium to arm at least two nuclear weapons if it is further enriched. Despite a drop in the number of centrifuges operating at Iran's uranium enrichment facility at Natanz, the Federation of American Scientists released a study on January 21 that warned that Iran's enrichment capacity has steadily increased and become more efficient.

The Need for Greater Sanctions

Washington should relentlessly ratchet up sanctions on Tehran also because rising oil prices have cushioned some of the impact of previous sanctions on Iran, which exports about 2.2 million barrels of crude per day. Iran earned about $64 billion from oil exports from January to November 2010, which was approximately $11 billion more than it earned over the entire year of 2009. Iran's regime, which has gorged itself on state-controlled oil revenues, is heavily dependent on oil profits to finance its military buildup and expensive nuclear program and minimize its need for popular support.

"Iranium," cartoon by Jan-Erik Ander (JEANDER). www.CartoonStock.com.

Sanctions can be helpful to the extent that they drive up the economic, diplomatic, and political costs that the regime must pay to continue on its present nuclear path. Although the regime is unlikely to halt its nuclear weapons program unless it is convinced that the consequences of continuing will threaten its hold on power, sanctions can also help fuel popular dissatisfaction with the regime that could eventually lead to a change of regime. Such a change would be the best possible outcome not only for American counter-proliferation, counter-terrorism, and human rights goals but also for the Iranian people.

What the Administration Should Do

To keep the pressure on Tehran, the Obama Administration should:

- *Push for more U.N. sanctions.* Washington should reject Tehran's claim, backed by Russian Foreign Minister

153

Sergey Lavrov before the Istanbul talks, that sanctions inhibit negotiations on an acceptable agreement with Iran. Sanctions clearly enhance international leverage over Tehran and give it strong incentives to negotiate a deal. Easing sanctions before Iran has complied with the U.N. Security Council resolutions would send a message of weakness and ambivalence that Tehran would exploit to buy more time for advancing its nuclear efforts. The U.S. should cite Iran's contemptuous stonewalling at the Istanbul talks as a clear indication that another round of U.N. sanctions is required. The new resolution should target Iranian officials responsible for human rights violations and restrict foreign investment, technology transfers, and technical assistance for Iran's energy sector—the regime's milk cow.

- *Ratchet up unilateral sanctions regimes against Iran.* While Russia and China are likely to dilute sanctions at the U.N. Security Council, much more can be done to increase pressure on Tehran outside the U.N. framework. Washington should press India, Pakistan, Turkey, and Persian Gulf states to ban foreign investment and technology transfers to Iran's energy sector as the U.S., Australia, Canada, the EU [European Union], Japan, and South Korea have already done to varying degrees. The U.S. should also press other countries to join in sanctioning foreign firms that export gasoline or refinery equipment to Iran, as the executive branch is authorized to do by the Comprehensive Iran Sanctions, Accountability and Divestment Act (CISADA) of 2010.

- *Strictly enforce U.S. sanctions.* Despite congressional authorization, the executive branch has failed to fully use its power to penalize foreign companies involved in Iran's energy sector, in part to avoid friction with allies.

The Obama Administration, which has sanctioned only one foreign company for violations of CISADA, needs to be more forward-leaning to enforce the sanctions. The Foundation for Defense of Democracies has identified more than 20 foreign companies involved in ongoing energy projects in Iran. Congress should exercise its oversight powers to ensure that existing sanctions laws are fully utilized to penalize Iran's dictatorship and its foreign enablers. Congress should also examine loopholes that previous Administrations have created to allow humanitarian aid, food, and medical supplies to be exported to Iran to ensure that such permitted exports are not funneled through companies controlled by Iran's Islamic Revolutionary Guard Corps.

- *Ensure that Chinese companies do not undercut sanctions.* In recent years, Chinese companies have developed extensive commercial ties with Iran. In particular, Chinese oil companies have assumed a growing share of foreign investment in Iran's energy sector, signing agreements to invest more than $100 billion there. The Obama Administration should press Beijing to rein in these companies and warn that Washington will impose sanctions on these companies if they follow through on those commitments with actual investments. Washington should also take action against any Chinese firms that seek to replace Japanese, South Korean, or Western firms that are pulling out of Iran.

Support for Iran's Opposition

Egypt's President Hosni Mubarak was forced out of power on the same day that Iran commemorates its 1979 revolution. But the two revolutions have important differences despite the cynical claims by Iran's tyrannical regime that Egyptians were inspired by Iran's Islamist revolution. In fact, Iran's opposition Green Movement has much more in common with Egypt's young protesters than the thuggish leaders of the regime, who have clamped down even harder on the leaders of the Green Movement to prevent them from demonstrating today in support of Egyptians, as they had planned.

Although the Obama Administration missed the opportunity to clearly state its support for Iran's opposition after it was galvanized by the stolen election of June 2009, it should now give at least as much rhetorical support to Iran's struggle for freedom as it did to Egypt's. Tehran's systematic repression of the political freedom and human rights of Iranian citizens deserves condemnation backed by international sanctions as much as Iran's nuclear defiance and support for terrorism.

"*These sanctions will harm the wrong people and have little impact on the political leadership.*"

Economic Sanctions on Iran Are Ineffective and Should Be Decreased

Joy Gordon

In the following viewpoint, Joy Gordon argues that economic sanctions on Iran by the United States and United Nations do more harm than good. Gordon claims that although recent sanctions are aimed at avoiding harm to the entire Iranian population, they actually are not so narrowly targeted. She contends that economic sanctions can create a humanitarian crisis and raise questions of justice when they punish ordinary citizens for the failures of their governments. Gordon is professor of philosophy at Fairfield University and senior fellow in the Global Justice Program at the MacMillan Center for International and Area Studies at Yale University. She is the author of Invisible War: The United States and the Iraq Sanctions.

Joy Gordon, "'Smart Sanctions' on Iran Are Dumb," *Foreign Policy in Focus*, September 9, 2010. www.fpif.org. Copyright © 2010 Institute for Policy Studies. All rights reserved. Reproduced by permission.

As you read, consider the following questions:

1. According to Gordon, what movement of the 1990s is aimed at targeting assets of political and military leaders without harming the general population?

2. The author claims that from the end of World War II to 1990 the United States has imposed what fraction of all global sanctions?

3. Gordon argues that economic sanctions against Iran are no more ethical or persuasive than economic sanctions leveled at what country?

In the face of the rising hysteria regarding Iran's development of its nuclear power facilities, there is talk of preemptive military strikes against Iran. Meanwhile, sanctions on Iran—by both the UN [United Nations] Security Council and the United States—have become increasingly harsh. And to the extent they are successful, these sanctions will harm the wrong people and have little impact on the political leadership.

Iran's Response to Sanctions

Yet another round of sanctions doesn't seem to have caused Iran to buckle. After the Security Council imposed new sanctions in June [2010], President Mahmoud Ahmadinejad compared the new resolutions to "a used handkerchief that should be thrown in the waste bin," and Iran's envoy to the IAEA [International Atomic Energy Agency] said that Iran's nuclear enrichment program "will not be suspended, even for a second."

Such responses are not surprising. In general sanctions do not work, in any regard. Almost invariably, they impact the poorest and most vulnerable, while the political and military leaders are insulated from their impact. Although the United States often views itself as providing a kind of moral leadership by sanctioning other nations, that view is almost never shared by the targeted population. Instead, sanctions trigger resentment and resistance among the population, and produces greater support for the government in the face of attacks from outside.

US Support for Smart Sanctions

The "smart sanctions" movement in the 1990s sought to focus on weapons, or the assets of political and military leaders, without harming the population as a whole. The U.S. claim to support only "smart sanctions" has certainly not been true with Iran. For example, the recent U.S. law refers to sanctions on Iran's oil and gas industries as "targeted," as though this is a narrow measure that will somehow not impact the entire population of Iran. But these industries account for one quarter of Iran's economy.

If the United States succeeded in shutting down the oil and gas industries, every aspect of life in Iran would be affected, far more than the impact of the 1973 Arab oil embargo on the United States. Eighty percent of the Iranian government's income comes from the energy sector. The government's extensive subsidies for food, gasoline, and housing—which, according to some estimates, account for over one-quarter of Iran's GDP [gross domestic product]—depend on this income. The United States is essentially attempting to bankrupt the state.

There is nothing "smart" about such a strategy. A similarly shortsighted approach in Iraq reduced funds for the military but also compromised all critical public services dependent on state funding. It led to layoffs of civil servants and the personnel staffing electricity generation, water treatment, and telephone systems. Teachers, doctors, educational supplies, and imported medicines for schools and health clinics were all at risk.

The Harmful Effects of UN Sanctions

The sanctions imposed on Iran by the UN Security Council, for which the United States has lobbied aggressively, are not much of an improvement over the U.S. government measures. The appendices attached to Security Council resolutions, which list the names of individual persons and companies, imply that the impact will be narrowly targeted. But, in fact, it is not.

UN sanctions, for instance, targeted Iran's Bank Mellat on the grounds that it facilitated financial transactions for military entities. But Bank Mellat is also one of the largest commercial banks in Iran, with over 1,800 branches and almost 25,000 employees. Bank Sepah, the fifth-largest bank in Iran, was also targeted, on the grounds that it "provides support" for Iran's Aerospace Industries Organization. It's as though Chase Manhattan Bank were prohibited from doing business, and had billions of dollars in international assets frozen, on the grounds that one of its clients is Sikorsky Aircraft, which makes military helicopters. This stands in marked contrast to actual targeted sanctions—for example, the boycott of Caterpillar, which makes the bulldozers that are directly used by Israel in the demolition of Palestinian homes.

The United States was also behind UN sanctions that target the Islamic Republic of Iran Shipping Lines (IRISL), on the grounds that it arranges shipments of cargo related to the military. But IRISL is also Iran's national shipping line. According to the U.S. Treasury Department, IRISL is "a global operator" that "provides a variety of maritime transport services" of every sort, "connect[ing] Iranian exporters and importers with South America, Europe, the Middle East, Asia, and Africa." And one-third of Iran's GDP consists of exports. To compromise Iran's major shipping lines would do damage far beyond blocking the transport of military items.

Iran's wealth and ingenuity at circumventing the sanctions have largely insulated it against the economic disruption that the sanctions are intended to bring about. But this isn't because the sanctions themselves are actually designed to avoid harming the innocent. To the contrary, they are aimed at undermining massive sectors of Iran's economy, and to the extent that they are successful, their harm will be indiscriminate.

The Problem with Sanctions

Economic sanctions have long been a favorite tool of the United States. From the end of World War II to 1990, the United States imposed two-thirds of all global sanctions, often acting unilaterally. U.S. policymakers were attracted to sanctions because they seem more substantial than "mere diplomacy," but without the risks and costs of military intervention. More importantly, this tool can do enormous harm to a country with a small or vulnerable economy and rarely contains the risk of reciprocal action against the U.S. economy (the Arab oil embargo of the 1970s was such an exception).

When Iraq invaded Kuwait, the United States pressed for the imposition of measures that would strangle Iraq's entire economy. When these sanctions were accompanied by the massive bombing campaign in 1991, which destroyed or crippled Iraq's infrastructure, from water treatment plants to roads and bridges, the result was a humanitarian crisis that never really abated. After the bombing, the sanctions prevented Iraq from restoring these capacities. Epidemics of cholera and typhoid continued for years. Malnutrition was widespread, and doctors had to treat diseases typically found in the poorest regions of the developing world. But, as with any economic crisis, the leadership didn't have to suffer the worst of the hardships. The hardest hit were the most vulnerable—the poor, the elderly, the sick, and infants and small children.

A Question of Justice

Sanctions that affect the fundamental economy of a nation raise questions of basic justice. How was it that an institution of global governance could punish those least responsible for

Iraq's military actions and political decisions, while the nation's political and military leadership, along with the economic elite, were insulated against these deprivations? In the face of the humanitarian catastrophe in Iraq, scholars and practitioners began formulating guidelines for "smart sanctions"— sanctions that would affect the political and military leaders without causing indiscriminate harm to the civilian population.

The U.S. measures against Iran, as well as those for which the United States aggressively advocates in international bodies, are no more ethical or persuasive than the devastating sanctions on Iraq. However much U.S. policymakers use lists of particular companies, or use terms like "smart" or "targeted," these measures are designed to cause hardship and deprivation for the innocent.

Truly smart sanctions on Iran wouldn't try to cripple the nation's energy industry, the nation's imports and exports, and the nation's access to the global financial system. Smart sanctions would target things like equipment specifically designed to convert domestic nuclear energy facilities to weapons production. But while the punitive measures continue to expand, the most promising of the diplomatic efforts, such as the compromise shaped by Turkey and Brazil, have been broken off. There may be something better than sanctions, or there may not. But at the very least, the Security Council and the United States should not create a situation that is worse than doing nothing at all.

> *"Appeals for more foreign aid, even when intended to promote the market, will continue to do more harm than good."*

US Foreign Aid Does More Harm Than Good

Ian Vasquez

In the following viewpoint, Ian Vasquez argues that there is widespread consensus that foreign aid does not support, but actually hinders, economic growth. Vasquez contends that transfers of aid from the developed to the developing world have financed governments who are responsible for their countries' impoverishment. In addition, he claims that foreign aid prevents governments from making needed market reforms. Furthermore, Vasquez claims that debt relief aid has been ineffective, because countries with forgiven debt are soon back for additional aid. Vasquez is director of the Cato Institute's Center for Global Liberty and Prosperity.

As you read, consider the following questions:

1. According to Vasquez, total foreign aid from rich countries totals approximately how much?

Ian Vasquez, "Foreign Aid and Economic Development," Chapter 63, in *Cato Handbook for Policymakers*, 7th Edition. Washington, DC: Cato Institute, 2009, pp. 655–660.

2. What two countries does the author give as examples of success stories, succeeding economically after US aid was cut off?

3. How much debt in poor countries was forgiven from 1989 to 1997, according to Vasquez?

In 2002, President [George W.] Bush called for increasing U.S. bilateral development assistance by about 50 percent by fiscal year 2006, gradually raising the aid above the then prevailing level of roughly $10 billion. The Millennium Challenge Account, managed by a new government agency, the Millennium Challenge Corporation, was created in 2004 to direct the additional funds to poor countries with sound policy environments. Likewise in recent years, the World Bank and the United Nations have been advocating a doubling of official development assistance worldwide to about $150 billion. Foreign aid has risen notably. The Bush administration reached its funding goal, and total aid from rich countries is now around $100 billion.

A Widespread Consensus About Aid

Those calls for significant increases in foreign aid are based on the argument that aid agencies have learned from the failure of past foreign aid programs and that overseas assistance can now be generally effective in promoting growth. But what we know about aid and development provides little reason for such enthusiasm:

- There is no correlation between aid and growth.

- Aid that goes into a poor policy environment doesn't work and contributes to debt.

- Aid conditioned on market reforms has failed.

- Countries that have adopted market-oriented policies have done so because of factors unrelated to aid.

- There is a strong relationship between economic freedom and growth.

A widespread consensus has formed about those points, even among development experts who have long supported government-to-government aid. As developing countries began introducing market reforms in the late 1980s and early 1990s, the most successful reformers also experienced noticeably better economic performance. As would be expected, the improvement among the successful reformers also improved the apparent performance of foreign aid in those countries—thus, the new emphasis on giving aid to countries that have already adopted good policies. The new approach to aid is dubious for many reasons, not the least of which is the fact that countries with sound policies will already be rewarded with economic growth and do not need foreign aid. In any event, much, if not most, foreign assistance will continue to be awarded without regard to the record of internal reform.

Aid to Governments

By the 1990s, the failure of conventional government-to-government aid schemes had been widely recognized and brought the entire foreign assistance process under scrutiny. For example, a [Bill] Clinton administration task force conceded that, "despite decades of foreign assistance, most of Africa and parts of Latin America, Asia and the Middle East are economically worse off today than they were 20 years ago." As early as 1989, a bipartisan task force of the House Foreign Affairs Committee concluded that U.S. aid programs "no longer either advance U.S. interests abroad or promote economic development." . . .

There are several reasons that massive transfers from the developed to the developing world have not led to a corresponding transfer of prosperity. Aid has traditionally been lent to governments, has supported central planning, and has been based on a fundamentally flawed vision of development.

By lending to governments, USAID [US Agency for International Development] and the multilateral development agencies supported by Washington have helped expand the state sector at the expense of the private sector in poor countries. U.S. aid to India from 1961 to 1989, for example, amounted to well over $2 billion, almost all of which went to the Indian state. Ghanaian-born economist George Ayittey complained that, as late as 1989, 90 percent of U.S. aid to sub-Saharan Africa went directly to governments.

Foreign aid has thus financed governments, both authoritarian and democratic, whose policies have been the principal cause of their countries' impoverishment. Trade protectionism, byzantine licensing schemes, inflationary monetary policy, price and wage controls, nationalization of industries, exchange-rate controls, state-run agricultural marketing boards, and restrictions on foreign and domestic investment, for example, have all been supported explicitly or implicitly by U.S. foreign aid programs.

Not only has lack of economic freedom kept literally billions of people in poverty, development planning has thoroughly politicized the economies of developing countries. Centralization of economic decisionmaking in the hands of political authorities has meant that a substantial amount of poor countries' otherwise useful resources have been diverted to unproductive activities, such as rent seeking by private interests or politically motivated spending by the state.

A Dismal Record

Research by economist Peter Boone of the London School of Economics confirms the dismal record of foreign aid to the developing world. After reviewing aid flows to more than 95 countries, Boone found that "virtually all aid goes to consumption" and that "aid does not increase investment and growth, nor benefit the poor as measured by improvements in human development indicators, but it does increase the size of

Aid to Africa

Giving alms to Africa remains one of the biggest ideas of our time—millions march for it, governments are judged by it, celebrities proselytize the need for it. . . .

Yet evidence overwhelmingly demonstrates that aid to Africa has made the poor poorer, and the growth slower. The insidious aid culture has left African countries more debt-laden, more inflation-prone, more vulnerable to the vagaries of the currency markets and more unattractive to higher-quality investment. It's increased the risk of civil conflict and unrest (the fact that over 60% of sub-Saharan Africa's population is under the age of 24 with few economic prospects is a cause for worry). Aid is an unmitigated political, economic and humanitarian disaster.

Dambisa Moyo,
"Why Foreign Aid Is Hurting Africa,"
Wall Street Journal, *March 21, 2009.*

government." A recent comprehensive study by the IMF [International Monetary Fund] also found no relationship between aid and growth.

It has become abundantly clear that as long as the conditions for economic growth do not exist in developing countries, no amount of foreign aid will be able to produce economic growth. Moreover, economic growth in poor countries does not depend on official transfers from outside sources. Indeed, were that not so, no country on earth could ever have escaped from initial poverty. The long-held premise of foreign assistance—that poor countries were poor because they lacked capital—not only ignored thousands of years of economic development history, it also was contradicted by contemporary events in the developing world, which saw the accumulation of massive debt, not development.

The Promotion of Market Reforms

Even aid intended to advance market liberalization can produce undesirable results. Such aid takes the pressure off recipient governments and allows them to postpone, rather than promote, necessary but politically difficult reforms. Ernest Preeg, former chief economist at USAID, for instance, noted that problem in the Philippines after the collapse of the [Ferdinand] Marcos dictatorship: "As large amounts of aid flowed to the [Corazon] Aquino government from the United States and other donors, the urgency for reform dissipated. Economic aid became a cushion for postponing difficult internal decisions on reform. A central policy focus of the Aquino government became that of obtaining more and more aid rather than prompt implementation of the reform program."

A similar outcome is evident in the Middle East, which receives about one-fifth to one-quarter of U.S. economic aid, most of which has historically been received by the governments of Egypt and Israel and, more recently, Iraq. It should not be surprising, then, that the region is notable for its low levels of economic freedom and little economic reform. In 1996, the Institute for Advanced Strategic and Political Studies, an Israeli think tank, complained: "Almost one-seventh of the [gross domestic product] comes to Israel as charity. This has proven to be economically disastrous. It prevents reform, causes inflation, fosters waste, ruins our competitiveness and efficiency, and increases the future tax burden on our children who will have to repay the part of the aid that comes as loans." In 2001, the institute again complained that foreign aid has "allowed Israel to avoid a very necessary liberalization of its state-controlled economy."

Far more effective at promoting market reforms is the suspension or elimination of aid. Although USAID lists South

Korea and Taiwan as success stories of U.S. economic assistance, those countries began to take off economically only after massive U.S. aid was cut off. As even the World Bank has conceded, "Reform is more likely to be preceded by a decline in aid than an increase in aid." When India faced Western sanctions in 1998 in response to nuclear tests there, the *International Herald Tribune* reported that "India approved at least 50 foreign-investment projects to compensate for the loss of aid from Japan and the United States" and that it would take additional measures to attract capital. In the end, the countries that have done the most to reform economically have made changes despite foreign aid, not because of it. . . .

The Cycle of Debt

Some 41 poor countries today suffer from inordinately high foreign debt levels. Thus, the World Bank and the IMF have devised a $68 billion debt-relief initiative for the world's heavily indebted poor countries. To fund this program, the aid agencies are requesting about half the money from the United States and other donors. The initiative, of course, is an implicit recognition of the failure of past lending to produce self-sustaining growth, especially since an overwhelming percentage of eligible countries' public foreign debt is owed to bilateral and multilateral lending agencies. Indeed, 96 percent of those countries' long-term debt is public or publicly guaranteed.

Forgiving poor nations' debt is a sound idea, on the condition that no other aid is forthcoming. Unfortunately, the multilateral debt initiative promises to keep poor countries on a borrowing treadmill, since they will be eligible for future multilateral loans based on conditionality. There is no reason, however, to believe that conditionality will work any better in the future than it has in the past. Again, as a recent World Bank study emphasized, "A conditioned loan is no guarantee that reforms will be carried out—or last once they are."

Nor is there reason to believe that debt relief will work better now than in the past. As former World Bank economist William Easterly has documented, donor nations have been forgiving poor countries' debts since the late 1970s, and the result has simply been more debt. From 1989 to 1997, 41 highly indebted countries saw some $33 billion of debt forgiveness, yet they still found themselves in an untenable position by the time the current round of debt forgiveness began. Indeed, they have been borrowing ever-larger amounts from aid agencies. Easterly notes, moreover, that private credit to the heavily indebted poor countries has been virtually replaced by foreign aid and that foreign aid itself has been lent on increasingly easier terms. Thus, when the World Bank and IMF call for debt forgiveness, it is the latest in a series of failed attempts by rich countries to resolve poor countries' debts.

At the same time, it has become increasingly evident that the debt-relief scheme is a financial shell game that allows the multilaterals to repay their previous loans without having to write down bad debt and thus without negatively affecting their financial status. If official donors wished to forgive debt, they could do so easily. Contributing money to the multilateral debt-relief initiative, however, will do little to promote reform or self-sustaining growth. . . .

Economic Freedom, Not Aid

Numerous studies have found that economic growth is strongly related to the level of economic freedom. Put simply, the greater a country's economic freedom, the greater its level of prosperity over time. Likewise, the greater a country's economic freedom, the faster it will grow. Economic freedom, which includes not only policies, such as free trade and stable money, but also institutions, such as the rule of law and the security of private property rights, increases more than income. It is also strongly related to improvements in other development indicators such as longevity, access to safe drinking water, lower corruption, and dramatically higher incomes for the poorest members of society.

Those developing countries, such as Chile, Estonia, and Taiwan, that have most liberalized their economies and achieved high levels of growth have done far more to reduce poverty and improve their citizens' standards of living than have foreign aid programs.

In the end, a country's progress depends almost entirely on its domestic policies and institutions, not on outside factors such as foreign aid. Congress should recognize that foreign aid has not caused the worldwide shift toward the market and that appeals for more foreign aid, even when intended to promote the market, will continue to do more harm than good.

> *"There are no sound indications that cuts or reductions in foreign assistance support are merited."*

US Foreign Aid Is Effective and Should Not Be Cut

Laurie A. Garrett

In the following viewpoint, Laurie A. Garrett argues that foreign assistance should not be cut. Garrett claims that US spending on human aid and development programs is much lower than most Americans believe it is but, nonetheless, such aid makes a big difference in relieving poverty and treating disease in the developing world. Furthermore, Garrett claims that there is no indication that a decrease in spending will be possible in the near future, because the need for such aid is high and the success of many programs has increased the demand for more aid. Garrett is a senior fellow for global health at the Council on Foreign Relations.

As you read, consider the following questions:

1. According to the author, what percentage of the US budget is spent on overseas health, development, and humanitarian and anti-poverty programs?

2. According to Garrett, how many fewer people died from malaria in 2008 than in 2000?

3. The author says that the Center for Strategic and International Studies suggests that by 2025 the United States spend how much per year on global health efforts?

Debate over the FY [fiscal year] 2011 federal budget has heightened in the Senate, as the Budget Committee voted on April 23 [2010] to cut foreign assistance spending by $4 billion—a 7 percent reduction in the already frugal White House proposed budget of $58.8 billion. Most of the budget is for nonmilitary programs in the frontline states, with less than a quarter—$14.6 billion—for global challenges like health, food security, climate change, and humanitarian assistance.

The White House, correctly, wants to maintain a strong commitment to overseas assistance and global health. Its budget request includes strategic and structural shifts to reach those goals, including aligning foreign assistance more closely with foreign policy objectives, demanding greater accountability from recipient governments, and delivering more "bang for the buck" by increasing cross-agency cooperation, streamlining delivery of goods and services, and reducing U.S. government redundancies.

US Spending on Foreign Aid

But while it's important to evaluate programs—and while questions of accountability and value loom large in the public's mind, especially at a time of concern about the economy—there are no sound indications that cuts or reductions in foreign assistance support are merited. These programs are saving and enhancing lives all over the world. Reductions in Account 150 spending (all spending on international programs by various departments and agencies) cannot possibly have a discernible impact on the federal budget deficit or the national debt, as the discretionary sums allotted to Account

150 are comparatively trivial. In fact, $14.6 billion for the abovementioned global challenges amounts to a mere .38 percent of the $3.8 trillion federal budget.

Here are some of the questions Congress is likely to look at as it considers the White House foreign assistance request.

What do American taxpayers and voters want the U.S. government to do in terms of foreign assistance?

Americans want to be magnanimous in helping poor nations but also want to reduce spending. The problem is that polls show that Americans actually believe that spending on overseas health, development, and humanitarian and anti-poverty programs is 15 to 20 percent of the national budget. In fact, spending has never exceeded 0.5 percent.

Very little of the government's budget is discretionary and easily cut, yet human aid and development programs are discretionary and also lack the strong constituency backing of other government programs. So these programs are vulnerable at a time when the global financial crisis, coming on the heels of the 2008 food and seed inflation, has greatly increased the need for agricultural, poverty, and health programs. Worse, World Bank estimates show backward movement on key health and development targets since the onset of the economic crisis. . . .

The Effectiveness of US Aid

Has increased American generosity over the last nine years made a difference?

Yes. Globally, funding for malaria control and treatment programs soared from $0.3 billion in 2003 to $1.7 billion in 2009, with the U.S. responsible for the lion's share of the effort. Worldwide, 1 million people died of malaria in 2000, while 860,000 died of the disease in 2008, according to the World Health Organization (WHO). About a third of the people in poor countries that need daily medicine to control HIV/AIDS are now receiving antiretroviral drugs with the

President's Emergency Plan for AIDS Relief (PEPFAR), the major provider of treatment. Mother and neonatal child survival has increased; more than a half million women died of childbirth related causes in 1980, while by 2008 that number was down to 343,000. The Bill and Melinda Gates Foundation, USAID [US Agency for International Development], UNICEF [United Nations Children's Fund], and the Global Alliance for Vaccines and Immunisation (GAVI) have pushed back mortality and sickness caused by diseases like polio, measles, diphtheria, rotaviruses, mumps, meningitis and the like. The WHO estimates that 4 million children were spared death from three diseases (Hepatitis B, Haemophilus influenzae type b and Pertussis) from 2001 to 2009, thanks to these vaccine efforts.

Still, there are real challenges ahead. The world economic crisis has forced millions of people into subsistence-level poverty and pushed back MDG [Millenium Development Goals] achievements. A World Bank report estimates, "An additional 55,000 infants might die in 2015. And 260,000 more children under five could have been prevented from dying in 2015 in the absence of the crisis. The cumulative total from 2009 to 2015 could reach 265,000 [infants] and 1.2 million [children under five]" due to economic setbacks in key countries.

Recipient governments and multilateral organizations are not prepared to take over management and financing of any major global health effort on their own. If support from the United States disappears or suffers a significant cutback, most health achievements face reversal, and "reversal" means deaths.

Reducing Dependence

A major concern of the [Barack] Obama administration's GHI [Global Health Initiative] is sustainability and exit strategies: Can programs be redesigned so that eventually countries and multilateral agencies will no longer be dependent on U.S. taxpayer support?

There is no evidence that the U.S. or other major donors will be able to decrease financial support of global health programs, in particular, without witnessing swift reversal of these achievements, because programs have lacked exit strategies and countries have insufficient resources and infrastructure to take on the projects. Even countries with extraordinary GDP [gross domestic product] growth, such as China, India, and Brazil, remain dependent on aid for health, and skew their priorities to reflect donor interests. Worse, many poor countries have decreased their contributions to government costs, writ large, and health specifically as they have absorbed greater quantities of donor support.

As the Obama administration tries to reform the coherence of U.S. aid programs, it should also look to improve their efficiency and lower administrative and contractor costs.

A Time of Need

Will America's partners in giving continue to carry their financial weight, both bilaterally and multilaterally?

Despite the world economic crisis, development aid rose in 2009, and most of the world's donors are on track to meet their basic 2010 commitments, according to OECD [Organisation for Economic Co-operation and Development]. In 2009, total donor support, including debt relief, hit $119.6 billion, a 0.7 percent increase over the previous year. Moreover, OECD says, "In 2009, net bilateral ODA [official development assistance] to Africa was USD [US dollars] 27 billion, representing an increase of 3 percent in real terms over 2008. USD 24 billion of this aid went to sub-Saharan Africa, an increase of 5.1 percent over 2008."

Many aid-dependent organizations and governments are experiencing shortfalls and budgetary woes, particularly in sectors related to the Millennium Development Goals, or MDGs. Overall, this appears to reflect failures to attain projected increases in support, rather than reductions in prior support levels. The most consistently cited example of this is PEPFAR.

The Demand for US Aid

Are the funding requests from the White House too large, or not large enough, in general or specifically?

Success breeds demand.

The Partnership for Maternal Newborn and Child Health says that G8 [the Group of Eight, a group representing eight major economies: France, Germany, Italy, Japan, the United Kingdom, the United States, Canada, and Russia] support must double this year, reaching $8 billion a year until 2015 in order to achieve the relevant MDGs, and then plateau in order to sustain the gains in lives saved.

GAVI desperately needs $4 billion in order to meet its 2010–2011 vaccination targets.

The Global Fund to Fight AIDS, Tuberculosis, and Malaria has committed billions more to needy countries than it actually has in the bank.

OXFAM [anti-poverty organization] is urging Congress to appropriate the White House-requested $3.5 billion for the Global Hunger and Food Security Initiative. The World Bank increased agricultural development investment from $4.1 billion in 2006 to $7.3 billion last year, but it needs more.

The Center for Strategic and International Studies convened a bipartisan Commission on Smart Global Health Policy that recently concluded that the United States should, from 2010 to 2025, aim to spend $25 billion per year by 2025 for global health efforts.

America embarked on a set of bold initiatives under President George W. Bush, aimed at reducing poverty and disease, especially in Africa. By the second Bush term these efforts, such as PEPFAR, the Millennium Challenge Corporation, and the President's Malaria Initiative, enjoyed strong bipartisan support. The Obama administration foreign assistance proposals should be viewed as a continuum in that arc of American diplomacy, generosity and strategic thinking: Abandoning it, for the sake of sparing less than 1/100th of the federal budget, makes no sense.

Periodical and Internet Sources Bibliography

The following articles have been selected to supplement the diverse views presented in this chapter.

Jagdish Bhagwati	"Banned Aid: Why International Assistance Does Not Alleviate Poverty," *Foreign Affairs*, January/February 2010.
Juan Cole	"Why Economic Sanctions on Iran Won't Work," *Salon*, April 19, 2010. www.salon.com.
Sandra I. Erwin	"Soldiers as Samaritans: What's the Right Balance?" *National Defense*, September 2008.
Richard Feinberg	"Haiti in the Balance: Why Foreign Aid Has Failed and What We Can Do About It," *Foreign Affairs*, May/June 2009.
Joseph Gerson	"10 Reasons to Withdraw U.S. Foreign Military Bases," *Peacework*, February 2007.
Richard N. Haass	"Enough Is Enough," *Newsweek*, February 1, 2010.
Shirl McArthur	"A Conservative Estimate of Total Direct U.S. Aid to Israel: Almost $114 Billion," *Washington Report on Middle East Affairs*, November 2008.
New African	"Was Aid to Ethiopia Diverted to Rebel Groups?" May 2010.
Josh Ruebner	"U.S. Can't Afford Military Aid to Israel," *Huffington Post*, February 26, 2010. www.huffingtonpost.com.
George Wedd	"Can Foreign Aid Ever Work?" *Contemporary Review*, Summer 2008.
DeWayne Wickham	"Dollars, Not Just Democracy, Often Drive U.S. Foreign Policy," *USA Today*, January 15, 2007.

 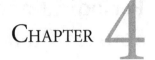

What Is the Global Impact of American Culture?

Chapter Preface

American culture is exported in many forms. Perhaps the most widely recognized influence is in entertainment: the American film industry has led the globe in export of films for decades, and American music—especially jazz, rock and roll, and blues—has had a profound effect on music produced all over the globe. America's cultural influence is not without controversy and, recently, one of the most controversial cultural exports is American eating habits. The export of American food products and the so-called Americanization of eating have been blamed for a wide variety of ills by other countries.

The US Centers for Disease Control and Prevention (CDC) notes, "During the past 20 years there has been a dramatic increase in obesity in the United States." In 2008, the CDC estimated that more than one-third of US adults were obese (at least 30 pounds overweight). Obesity contributes to a variety of health problems, such as high cholesterol, high blood pressure, diabetes, cancer, and heart disease. The World Cancer Research Fund warned, "The 'Americanization' of British eating habits is a serious public health threat."[1] In particular, the group blamed the American trend of "super-sized" portions as leading to an increase in obesity. The concern about a rise in obesity is not limited to Great Britain. In France, some claim that the Americanization of eating habits, such as snacking, has led to an increase in childhood obesity. In response to the problem, France has banned all vending machines that sell candy and soft drinks in schools.

The export of American restaurants has resulted in the growth of fast-food empires internationally. American restaurants such as McDonald's, Burger King, and KFC are now

---

1. Mike Wendling, "'Americanization' of British Food Blamed for Obesity," *CNSnews .com*, July 7, 2008. http://www.cnsnews.com/news/article/14663.

found across the globe. Writer Danny Duncan Collum claims that the proliferation of American fast food is increasing obesity rates worldwide: "Wherever our fast-food chains establish a presence, increases in the percentage of people who are overweight follow."[2] The presence of McDonald's in France has had mixed responses. A 1999 farmers' union demonstration in Southern France against the McDonald's resulted in $150,000 in damage. But little more than a decade later, there are more than 1,000 McDonald's locations in France.

The export of American culture worldwide often is plagued by paradox. On the one hand, American culture is popular so it ends up everywhere. On the other hand, its ubiquity makes it a frequent target of criticism, especially because many other cultures perceive elements of American culture as replacing their own. Nonetheless, as long as there is a demand for American cultural products overseas, the export of American culture—along with the controversy—will likely continue.

2. Danny Duncan Collum, "Our Fast-Food Empire," *Sojourners*, May 2006, p. 41.

| "*People abroad are increasingly indiffer-ent to America's culture.*"

American Culture Is No Longer the Dominant Culture in the World

Richard Pells

In the following viewpoint, Richard Pells argues that the global interest in American culture has declined from its apex in the early twentieth century. He contends that the current place of American culture as just one culture among many is mainly explained by globalization. Pells claims that the decentralization of knowledge and culture brought about by globalization has strengthened the impact of cultures outside the United States, resulting in a world of cultural pluralism. Pells is professor of history at the University of Texas at Austin. He is the author of Modernist America: Art, Music, Movies, and the Globalization of American Culture.

As you read, consider the following questions:

1. The author claims that the 1960s radio show *Music USA* had how many listeners around the globe?

Richard Pells, "Does the World Still Care About American Culture?" *Chronicle of Higher Education*, vol. 55, March 6, 2009, pp. B4–B5. Copyright © 2009 by The Chronicle of Higher Education. Reproduced by permission of the author.

2. According to Pells, the American share of movie ticket sales in France dropped by how many percentage points from 1998 to 2008?

3. Why have cell phones and the Internet made American culture less relevant, according to the author?

For most of the 20th century, the dominant culture in the world was American. Now that is no longer true. What is most striking about attitudes toward the United States in other countries is not the anti-Americanism they reflect, or the disdain for former President George W. Bush, or the opposition to American foreign policies. Rather, people abroad are increasingly indifferent to America's culture.

Global Interest in American Culture

American culture used to be the elephant in everyone's living room. Whether people felt uncomfortable with the omnipresence of America's high or popular culture in their countries, they could not ignore its power or its appeal. American writers and artists were superstars—the objects of curiosity, admiration, and envy. Today they are for the most part unnoticed, or regarded as ordinary mortals, participants in a global rather than a distinctively American culture.

America's elections still matter to people overseas. As someone who has taught American studies in Europe, Latin America, and Asia, I received e-mail messages from friends abroad asking me who I thought would win the presidency in November [2008]. But I rarely get queries about what I think of the latest American movie. Nor does anyone ask me about American novelists, playwrights, composers, or painters.

American Culture in History

Imagine any of these events or episodes in the past happening now: In 1928, fresh from having written "Rhapsody in Blue" and the "Piano Concerto in F Major," George Gershwin traveled to Paris and Vienna. He was treated like an idol. As

The Declining Influence of American Culture

The "newness" of American cultural products, their greatest drawing card in the past, is increasingly fading worldwide. . . .

To be sure, there are cultural artifacts originating from America that to others still reveal undiscovered shores. But in an information-saturated world more superficially knowledgeable about the U.S. than ever before, no American cultural product today—for better or for worse—comes close to matching the initial impact on global audiences of twentieth-century American music, movies, pulp fiction, clothes, ads and fast food.

John H. Brown,
"Is the U.S. High Noon Over? Reflections on the
Declining Global Influence of American Popular Culture,"
English (Journal for Russian Teachers of English), no. 7,
February 2004.

America's most famous composer, he met with many of the leading European modernists [Austrian composer Arnold] Schoenberg, [Russian composer Igor] Stravinsky, [Russian composer Sergei] Prokofiev, [French composer Maurice] Ravel. At one point, Gershwin asked Stravinsky if he could take lessons from the great Russian. Stravinsky responded by asking Gershwin how much money he made in a year. Told the answer was in six figures, Stravinsky quipped, "In that case, . . . I should study with you."

In the 1930s, Louis Armstrong and Duke Ellington toured throughout Europe, giving concerts to thousands of adoring fans, including members of the British royal family. In the 1940s and 50s, Dave Brubeck, Miles Davis, Dizzy Gillespie, Benny Goodman, and Charlie Parker often gave concerts in

Western and Eastern Europe, the Soviet Union, the Middle East, Africa, Asia, and Latin America. The Voice of America's most popular program in the 1960s was a show called *Music USA*, specializing in jazz, with an estimated 100 million listeners around the world. In the 1940s and 50s as well, Leonard Bernstein was invited to conduct symphony orchestras in London, Moscow, Paris, Prague, Tel Aviv, and the La Scala opera house, in Milan.

If you were a professor of modern literature at a foreign university, your reading list had to include [Saul] Bellow, [John] Dos Passos, [William] Faulkner, [Ernest] Hemingway, and [John] Steinbeck. If you taught courses on the theater, it was obligatory to discuss *Death of a Salesman*, *The Iceman Cometh*, *Long Day's Journey Into Night*, and *A Streetcar Named Desire*.

If you wanted to study modern art, you did not—like Gene Kelly in *An American in Paris*—journey to the City of Light (all the while singing and dancing to the music of Gershwin) to learn how to become a painter. Instead you came to New York, to sit at the feet of Willem de Kooning and Jackson Pollock. Or later you hung out at Andy Warhol's "factory," surrounded by celebrities from the arts and the entertainment world.

If dance was your specialty, where else could you find more creative choreographers than Bob Fosse or Jerome Robbins? If you were an aspiring filmmaker in the 1970s, the movies worth seeing and studying all originated in America. What other country could boast of such cinematic talent as Woody Allen, Robert Altman, Francis Ford Coppola, George Lucas, Martin Scorsese, and Steven Spielberg?

One Culture Among Many

Of course, there are still American cultural icons who mesmerize a global audience or whose photos are pervasive in the pages of the world's tabloid newspapers. Bruce Springsteen can always pack an arena wherever he performs. The Broadway musical *Rent* has been translated into more than 20 languages. Hollywood's blockbusters still make millions of dollars abroad. America's movie stars remain major celebrities at international film festivals.

But there is a sense overseas today that America's cultural exports are not as important, or as alluring, as they once were. When I lecture abroad on contemporary American culture, I find that few of America's current artists and intellectuals are household names, luminaries from whom foreigners feel they need to learn. The cultural action is elsewhere—not so much in Manhattan or San Francisco but in Berlin (the site of a major film festival) and Mumbai (the home of Indian filmmakers and media entrepreneurs who are now investing in the movies of Spielberg and other American directors). The importance of Mumbai was reinforced, spectacularly, when *Slumdog Millionaire* won the Oscar for best picture.

The Impact of Globalization

What accounts for the decline of interest in American art, literature, and music? Why has American culture become just another item on the shelves of the global supermarket?

The main answer is that globalization has subverted America's influence. During the 1990s, many people assumed that the emergence of what they called a global culture was just another mechanism for the "Americanization" of the world. Be it Microsoft or McDonald's, Disney theme parks or shopping malls, the movies or the Internet, the artifacts of American culture seemed ubiquitous and inescapable.

Yet far from reinforcing the impact of American culture, globalization has strengthened the cultures of other nations, regions, and continents. Instead of defining what foreigners want, America's cultural producers find themselves competing with their counterparts abroad in shaping people's values and tastes. What we have in the 21st century is not a hegemonic [meaning predominant influence over others] American culture but multiple forms of art and entertainment—voices, images, and ideas that can spring up anywhere and be disseminated all over the planet.

American television programs like *Dallas* and *Dynasty* were once the most popular shows on the airwaves, from Norway to New Zealand. Now many people prefer programs that are locally produced. Meanwhile cable and satellite facilities permit stations like [Arabic news outlet] Al-Jazeera to define and interpret the news from a Middle Eastern perspective for people throughout the world.

Since 2000, moreover, American movies have steadily lost market share in Europe and Asia. In 1998, the year in which *Titanic* was released abroad, American films commanded 64 percent of the ticket sales in France. Ten years later, Hollywood's share of the French market has fallen to 50 percent. Similarly, in 1998, American films accounted for 70 percent of the tickets sold in South Korea. Today that figure has fallen to less than 50 percent. As in the case of television programs, audiences increasingly prefer movies made in and about their own countries or regions. Indian films are now more popular in India than are imports from Hollywood. At the same time, American moviegoers are increasingly willing to sample films from abroad (and not just in art houses), which has led to the popularity in the United States of Japanese cartoons and animated films as well as recent German movies like *The Lives of Others*.

The Decentralization of Culture

After World War II, professors and students from abroad were eager to study in the United States. America was, after all, the center of the world's intellectual and cultural life. Now, with the rise of continental exchange programs and the difficulties that foreign academics face obtaining U.S. visas, it is often easier for a Dutch student to study in Germany or France, or for a Middle Eastern student to study in India, than for either of them to travel to an American university. That further diminishes the impact of American culture abroad.

Crowds, especially of young people, still flock to McDonald's—whether in Beijing, Moscow, or Paris. But every country has always had its own version of equally popular fast food. There are wurst stands in Germany and Austria, fish-and-chips shops in England, noodle restaurants in South Korea and Singapore, kabob outlets on street corners in almost any city (including in America), all of which remain popular and compete effectively with the Big Mac.

Finally, cellphones and the Internet make information and culture instantly available to anyone, without having to depend any longer on American definitions of what it is important to know. Indeed, globalization has led not to greater intellectual and political uniformity but to the decentralization of knowledge and culture. We live today in a universe full of cultural options, and we are therefore free to choose what to embrace and what to ignore.

I am not suggesting that America's culture is irrelevant. It remains one—but only one—of the cultural alternatives available to people abroad and at home. Moreover, it is certainly conceivable that President [Barack] Obama will improve America's currently dreadful image in the world, encouraging people to pay more attention not only to American policies but also to American culture—which the Bush administration, despite its efforts at cultural diplomacy, was never able to do.

But it is doubtful that America will ever again be the world's pre-eminent culture, as it was in the 20th century. That is not a cause for regret. Perhaps we are all better off in a world of cultural pluralism than in a world made in America.

"Whatever their common roots, pornography and Puritanism produce very different sorts of anti-Americanism."

The Widespread Export of American Culture Leads to Anti-Americanism

The Economist

In the following viewpoint, The Economist claims anti-Americanism around the globe has its roots in two very different sources. According to the author, the first source of anti-Americanism, found widely in Europe, is America's religiosity. The author claims that the second source, found in the Muslim world, is American culture. Both America's Pentecostalism and American pop culture are aggressively exported, claims the author, leading to an export of American culture wars between what the author calls the Puritans and the pornographers. The Economist is a global newspaper of analysis and opinion.

As you read, consider the following questions:

1. According to the author, what percentage of Americans believe in God?

Economist, "Puritans or Pornographers? The Schizophrenia at the Heart of Anti-Americanism," vol. 378, February 25, 2006, p. 42. Copyright © 2006 The Economist Newspaper Limited. All rights reserved. Reproduced by permission.

2. *The Economist* claims that what percentage of Pakistanis admit to enjoying American films and music?

3. How many American missionaries are there around the world, according to *The Economist*?

Foreigners, argues [American sociologist] Mr [Peter] Berger, have oddly confused views of America as a land of "Puritans and pornographers"—and that confusion makes fighting anti-Americanism extremely difficult.

The Roots of Anti-Americanism

"Puritans and pornographers" is a caricature, of course. But provided you adopt a broad definition of both Puritanism and pornography—with Puritanism standing for religion and pornography standing for popular culture—it is not an absurd one. America is a strikingly effective producer of popular culture. It not only makes more of it than any other country; it also produces more in-your-face culture—loud mouthed, libidinous and impossible to ignore. Yet it also stands out from other developed countries when it comes to resisting secularisation. America is the only modern country where most people belong to a religious organisation and where some 90% believe in God.

Arguably, America's religiosity and its popular culture spring from the same commitment to free markets. Its churches, no less than its film studios, have thrived precisely because they have never been shackled to the state and thus have to compete for customers. But whatever their common roots, pornography and Puritanism produce very different sorts of anti-Americanism.

Disdain of Religiosity and Culture

For many Euro-secularists, America's religiosity is its least attractive characteristic. They can't believe that any modern person can be religious unless they are either stupid (Britain's

Views of American Exports

| | Positive views of ... | |
	US movies, music, & TV	Spread of US ideas*
Canada	73	22
Argentina	50	10
Bolivia	49	19
Brazil	69	23
Chile	58	24
Mexico	53	23
Peru	50	29
Venezuela	71	37
Britain	63	21
France	65	18
Germany	62	17
Italy	66	25
Spain	72	16
Sweden	77	28
Bulgaria	51	25
Czech Republic	58	20
Poland	65	23
Russia	38	14
Slovakia	61	23
Ukraine	47	20
Turkey	22	4
Egypt	39	13
Jordan	40	12

* "Good that American ideas and customs are spreading here."

SOURCE: Pew Research Center, "Pew Global Attitudes Project: Spring 2007 Survey," 2007.

[CONTINUED]

Views of American Exports

	Positive views of …	
	US movies, music, & TV	Spread of US ideas*
Kuwait	53	10
Lebanon	71	38
Morocco	42	12
Palestinian ter.	23	3
Israel	72	56
Pakistan	4	4
Bangladesh	14	25
Indonesia	50	11
Malaysia	54	16
China	42	38
India	23	29
Japan	70	42
South Korea	49	38
Ethiopia	58	54
Ghana	54	43
Ivory Coast	86	79
Kenya	51	45
Mali	68	45
Nigeria	59	51
Senegal	62	32
South Africa	70	41
Tanzania	29	12
Uganda	54	45

* "Good that American ideas and customs are spreading here."

SOURCE: Pew Research Center, "Pew Global Attitudes Project: Spring 2007 Survey," 2007.

Private Eye dubs George [W.] Bush the leader of the "Latter Day Morons") or insane (a former German chancellor was known to accuse Mr Bush of "hearing voices"). The Pew Research Centre's survey of global attitudes last year [2005] discovered that most French and Dutch, as well as pluralities of Britons and Germans, think America is too religious.

Yet many cultural conservatives dislike America for exactly the opposite reason—because it is a battering ram for popular culture. A few Muslims worry that America is a "Crusader state", engaged in a religious war with Islam (a worry not helped by the suggestion after September 11th [2001 terrorist attacks] from one conservative pundit, Ann Coulter: "We should invade their countries, kill their leaders, and convert them to Christianity"). But most Muslims, and quite a number of traditional Europeans, worry far more about America's version of Mammon [the god of wealth] than about its version of God.

In some parts of the Muslim world, majorities admit to enjoying American films and music (though in Pakistan only 4% admit to such cravings). But majorities also tell Pew's researchers that they are worried about American values and lifestyles. This plays on two deep-seated worries about American popular culture: that it is hard to filter so that you just get the good bits (download Bob Dylan on to your son's iPod, and Snoop Dogg soon pops up as well) and that popular culture spawns social change. Children end up hanging around at the mall or at McDonald's rather than coming home for dinner.

The Export of American Culture Wars

What makes the "pornography" and the Puritanism so hard to take for foreigners is that America is so aggressive at exporting both of them. With pop culture, this is well documented. The perennial tedium of the Oscars [awards] ceremony won't prevent millions of people from watching it. But America is also a world-beater when it comes to exporting religion. Pentecostalism, which started off at a Bible college in Topeka, Kansas, in 1901, is now the world's fastest-growing religion, with 500m [500 million] followers. There are more than 140,000 American missionaries around the world and American-style megachurches are beginning to appear in Europe. Meanwhile, in Congress, evangelicals are taking the lead in shaping American policy on aid and human rights.

One way of looking at this is that Mr [James] Hunter's culture wars [term invented by Hunter] are now going global. That is partly because the battles between pornographers and Puritans in America rivet outsiders: who could not fail to be interested in the Kansas attorney-general who wants to be informed whenever there is "compelling evidence" of sexual interaction involving teenagers in his state? But there is also a deeper reason: many other countries are having to grapple with the problems America has.

This may be most obvious in the developing world, where traditional societies will inevitably have to endure their own version of America's culture wars as they get richer. But secular Europe has also recently discovered that it has not "outgrown" religious conflict—whether it be Christians complaining about the blasphemous BBC [British Broadcasting Corporation] or the continent's ever larger and more assertive Muslim population complaining about cartoons. As in so many other aspects of anti-Americanism, the schizophrenic fury against pornographers and Puritans is a twisted compliment; America is once again leading the way.

> *"The assumption among Americans that people from other cultures are becoming 'just like us' ... is leading to many cultural misunderstandings."*

The Existence of a Uniform Global Material Culture Masks Differences

Luis Martinez-Fernandez

In the following viewpoint, Luis Martinez-Fernandez contends that the spread of a uniform, largely American, material culture around the globe can lead to cultural misunderstandings. Martinez-Fernandez claims that beneath the surface of this material culture, people still retain their own cultural values. Americans, in particular, he claims, misunderstand the adoption of American material culture as an adoption of American values. Martinez-Fernandez concludes that Americans need to develop better cultural literacy in order to thrive in relationships with non-Americans. Martinez-Fernandez is a professor of history at the University of Central Florida.

Luis Martinez-Fernandez, "Just Like Us? Not Likely," *Chronicle of Higher Education*, vol. 53, December 8, 2006. Copyright © 2006 by The Chronicle of Higher Education. Reproduced by permission of the author.

As you read, consider the following questions:

1. How many words are in the English language, according to Martinez-Fernandez?

2. According to the author, the National Geographic Society found that what percentage of Americans could not find the United States on a map?

3. Martinez-Fernandez claims there are how many Hispanics and Latinos in the United States who speak Spanish?

Growing international competition from the European Union, China, India, and other countries has created urgent challenges for the United States. How well this country will fare in the new global reality will no longer depend on American political influence, military might, or capacity to expand economic productivity. Instead, leaders of American institutions and business organizations will need to acquire, develop, and master international cultural fluency.

The Global Material Culture

The world is moving toward a uniform material culture, dominated by mostly material American influences: technological innovations, fashion, Hollywood and the celebrity culture it promotes, hip-hop, and rock 'n' roll. But the pervasiveness of the trappings of American culture obscures the central cultural paradox that lies within the globalization process: Although people around the world may wear, eat, and listen to American products, they continue to maintain their deeply ingrained values, beliefs, and underlying assumptions. They may embrace the material products of modernity, but they cling tenaciously to their underlying cultural cores—which remain vibrant and resiliently distinct.

For example, an Andalusian businessman may purchase the most precise Swiss watch on the market, but that does not mean that he will be bound by the notions of punctuality—

rigidity, if you ask him—that regiment the lives of northern Europeans. Conservative Islamic individuals may welcome Western technology but also reject secularism, Western democratic practices, and notions of gender equality.

The New Culture Hybrids

In fact, new forms of cultural hybrids have surfaced as the bedrock values and beliefs of the world's cultures sport the veneer of an increasingly visible—and audible—North American material culture. For example, a person whose native language is not English can adopt the English language as a means of communication for a variety of reasons, including the desire to reach a broader audience or the need to use a more precise language with a richer vocabulary. (English has about 900,000 words, while French, for example, has fewer than 100,000.) Yet that same person will most likely retain his or her own cultural identity as a writer. Thus a Cuban author, like me, may write in English while maintaining a Cuban voice, working with a particular palette of symbols, themes, rhythms, forms of irony, and humor that is characteristic of Cuban literature.

Another example: Four Spaniards may have lunch at the McDonald's in Madrid's *Gran Via*. They may consume Big Macs, French fries, and what passes for milkshakes. But at the same time, they will probably practice the various rituals and meanings associated with eating out in Spain. They will eat as a social, rather than an individual, activity. They will have a later, longer, nonrushed meal, perhaps followed by a siesta. The person who invited the others will pay for the meal. They will never go Dutch, and rarely will they let a woman pick up the check. And they will never, God forbid, take out a calculator at the register to divide the tab equally.

The same phenomenon occurs with music. In the United States, the Walkman and the iPod are the symbols and technologies of an individualistic enjoyment of music. In contrast,

The Significance of American Consumer Culture

Even though American consumer culture is widespread, its significance is often exaggerated. You can choose to drink Coke and eat at McDonald's without becoming American in any meaningful sense. One newspaper photo of Taliban fighters in Afghanistan showed them toting Kalashnikovs [rifles]—as well as a sports bag with Nike's trademark swoosh. People's culture—in the sense of their shared ideas, beliefs, knowledge, inherited traditions, and art—may scarcely be eroded by mere commercial artifacts that, despite all the furious branding, embody at best flimsy values.

Philippe Legrain,
"Cultural Globalization Is Not Americanization,"
Chronicle of Higher Education, *May 9, 2003.*

a middle-class Angolan teenager may purchase a CD of American rock 'n' roll yet probably play that music in a communal fashion, with several people listening, dancing, or singing along.

The Danger of Cultural Misunderstandings

The assumption among Americans that people from other cultures are becoming "just like us" simply because they use the same products or wear the same clothes is leading to many cultural misunderstandings. Almost everyone knows that saying "Can you please pass the jelly?" (instead of "jam") while having tea in London may lead to faintings among one's table mates. But are we aware that if we are invited to dinner in an Arab home and bring food or a bottle of wine, it will be offensive—not only because Islam condemns the consumption

199

of alcoholic beverages, but also because the gift implies that the hosts cannot afford to provide the meal? Or that while direct and assertive conversations are generally used while conducting business in the United States, that style is deemed inappropriate and rude by Japanese businessmen? Or that Hispanic people are less likely to say no to an invitation, because refusing it—regardless of whether or not they plan to attend—would be discourteous?

Even with the United States' success in spreading its material culture throughout the world, such underlying values, mores, and habits persist. Being unaware of that—that is, lacking international cultural fluency—will hurt Americans both individually and as a country, whether we are trying to seal a business deal with Mexican executives, penetrate the Vietnamese consumer market in Los Angeles, or build a real coalition for war or peace in the Middle East.

A Lack of Skills Among Americans

What's more, the majority of Americans lack basic foreign-language skills. In past decades, the nation's government, business, and intellectual leaders were ill prepared to face the linguistic challenges of having Russian-speaking foes and of sharing the hemisphere with Spanish- and Portuguese-speaking neighbors. More recently the grave scarcity of fluent Arab-language interpreters and translators in the FBI [Federal Bureau of Investigation], the military, and the State Department has cost the nation dearly, hampering its fight against Islamic terrorists and Iraqi insurgents.

The extent of geographic illiteracy among American students and the general population is notorious and embarrassing. Survey after survey has demonstrated that students and people in general in the United States rank near the bottom compared with their counterparts from other industrialized countries. This year [2006] the National Geographic Society released the results of a survey showing that only a quarter of

Americans between the ages of 18 and 24 could identify Iran or Israel on a map, only 36 percent could find England, and, incredibly, 6 percent could not even find the United States.

How do we prepare the United States and its citizens for continuing and growing challenges of globalization? The voting booth might be a good place to start. We should reject political candidates and leaders who cast their opponents' cosmopolitan experiences and sensitivities as almost unpatriotic. During the 2004 presidential campaign, for instance, Republicans painted the Democratic candidate, Sen. John Kerry, as dangerously Europeanized because he had studied abroad, spoke several languages, and played classical guitar.

We should also seek to reform our schools and colleges. Unfortunately, students in elementary and secondary education are taught to pass standardized tests but are not prepared to pass life tests that require communicating across cultures. Our K-12 and higher-education systems should do a much better job of producing graduates who are not only multilingual but also fluent in cultural and geographic literacy.

The Importance of Cultural Literacy

While English is the world's *lingua franca* [common language], the mastery of foreign languages is essential for the international exchange of products and ideas. As I recently heard someone put it, "If you want to buy anything from anywhere in the world, you can manage with only English; if you want to sell something abroad, you'd better learn the language of your targeted customers."

In these times of marked—perhaps obsessive—emphasis on math and science education, colleges should strengthen their language requirements to produce graduates who can communicate and function effectively in an increasingly globalized world and a multilingual country. We should, for example, start teaching Chinese in school and college, and expand opportunities for students to master the Spanish language, spoken by close to 40 million Hispanics and Latinos in the United States.

Likewise study-abroad programs should be democratized and made more affordable, so that more students can include such experiences as part of their higher education. Paradoxically, and unfortunately, as the importance of multilingual skills and international cultural fluency expands, the role of the humanities and social sciences continues to erode within most American colleges as resources are redirected toward the hard sciences, engineering, and the health sciences.

American institutions—whether the State Department, Wal-Mart, *The New York Times*, or the local community college—can also do their part by hiring and further training internationally fluent decision makers, skilled at navigating the challenging waters of our diverse nation and globalized world. College graduates with degrees in the humanities and social sciences, and people from diverse linguistic and cultural backgrounds, are best suited to play the role of interlocutors and cultural translators. Ignoring or underutilizing their skills and knowledge will hurt the nation in the marketplace of goods and services, as well as in the global marketplace of ideas.

│ *"America's narrative, which has waxed for so long, is now waning in its universal appeal."*

The Export of American Culture Is Increasingly Harming America's Reputation

Mortimer B. Zuckerman

In the following viewpoint, Mortimer B. Zuckerman claims that the way America is portrayed through its pop culture exports has a profound effect on the global opinion of the United States. Zuckerman contends that Hollywood has long been the main disseminator of the American narrative and historically has made films that show good insight into American ideals. Zuckerman expresses concern that recently the goal of commercial success has caused an increase in American media that is losing its appeal and negatively impacting America's global reputation. Zuckerman is editor-in-chief of US News & World Report.

As you read, consider the following questions:

1. Zuckerman claims that the message from American pop culture has long reflected what value?

Mortimer B. Zuckerman, "What Sets Us Apart," *US News & World Report*, vol. 141, July 3, 2006, p. 72. Copyright © 2006 US News & World Report, L.P. All rights reserved. Reproduced by permission.

2. According to the author, what is the reason Hollywood has been offering more dumbed-down blockbuster films?

3. The author points to what four regions of the world where favorable opinion of the United States has dropped dramatically?

The only things that "every community in the world from Zanzibar to Hamburg recognizes in common" are American cultural artifacts—the jeans and the colas, the movies and the TV sitcoms, the music, and the rhetoric of freedom. That observation was made 65 years ago by Henry Luce in his essay "The American Century," but—to paraphrase President [Ronald] Reagan—Luce hadn't seen anything yet. We have lived through an astounding acceleration in the dissemination of American cultural values with profound implications for the rest of the world. As Plato is widely quoted as having said, "Those who tell the stories rule society."

The Message in American Pop Culture

Our storytellers—encapsulated in the one word *Hollywood*—make up a significant piece of America's "soft power." Through the media's projection of the American narrative, the world gets some pretty good insight into America's ideals. Most of the time, since World War II, we have reflected the rule of law, individual freedom, defense of human rights, and the just use of American power against fascism and communism. The American narrative, as portrayed, say, by Jimmy ("aw shucks") Stewart in the Frank Capra classic *It's a Wonderful Life*, enchanted the world.

The message from American pop culture has long been anti-authoritarian, challenging power in ways unthinkable in many countries. The hero, going up against the odds, projected a populist narrative that celebrated the common decencies against the wicked authorities or the excesses of capital-

ism. Millions who saw such films around the globe derived a sense of phantom citizenship in America, an appetite for the life that only liberty can bring.

The Downside of Commercial Success

The universality of the commercial appeal was due in part to Hollywood's munificent creative and marketing skills, but also fundamentally in the fact that we are such a richly heterogeneous society that our exports had been pretested at home. Hollywood supplies over 70 percent of the European film markets and 90 percent of those of the rest of the world, with the possible exception of India. To reach the younger populations under the age of 25, who constitute the bulk of the moviegoing audience, Hollywood has been offering more dumbed-down blockbusters based on action, violence, sex, and special effects like *Jurassic Park*. Such films travel more easily than movies with subtle dialogue or predominantly American references, like *Forrest Gump*. For similar reasons, comedy was structured to hinge on crude slapstick rather than situational wit and wordplay.

The underside of this commercial success is the cultural deficit of associating America with crime, vacuity, moral decay, promiscuity, and pornography—a trend that also worries American parents; Asian and Muslim worlds are already in revolt against it, but also against the libertarian and secular messages of American media. Our media project defiance and ridicule not just of illegitimate authority but of any authority at all—parents, teachers, and political leaders. Even in the West this elicits as much loathing as love. Abroad, it may make dictatorship more difficult, but it also makes democracy less attractive. These images have contributed to make *Americanization* a dirty word, with the American lifestyle and American capitalism widely viewed as an anarchic revolutionary force. It is perceived as trampling social order in the ruthless pursuit of profits, creating a new class system, based on money, combined with an uninhibited pursuit of pleasure and a disordered sense of priorities in which the needs of the less successful are neglected. What's more, America is increasingly seen as certain of its own righteousness, justifying the use of force to impose American views and values.

Opinion of the United States

So America's narrative, which has waxed for so long, is now waning in its universal appeal. Witness the decline of America's image abroad. In the most recent Pew Research Center poll, favorable opinion of the United States has fallen in most of the 14 countries surveyed, dropping dramatically in Europe, India, and Indonesia, but especially in the Middle East. The main provocation is the war in Iraq. It made anti-Americanism respectable again and crystallized long-standing grievances over American environmental policy and perceived support for globalization, multinational corporations, the death penalty, and friendly authoritarian governments around the world.

These perceptions are badly skewed. They fail to do justice to what is so wonderful about the United States: its individualism, its embrace of diversity, its opportunities for freedom, the welcome it extends to newcomers, and the uniqueness of an entrepreneurial, pragmatic society that is dramatically open to energy and talent. No other country provides the environment for self-help, self-improvement, and self-renovation. No other country possesses our unique mood of buoyancy, optimism, and confidence for the future.

How we portray ourselves positively (while not ignoring the warts) is a challenge to our creative talents—and to all of us.

"Any new investment in American 'smart power' should include a substantial cultural component."

America Could Improve Its Image by Exporting Finer Cultural Entertainment

Martha Bayles

In the following viewpoint, Martha Bayles argues that America's declining reputation can be improved by exporting more serious forms of entertainment. Bayles contends that the distorted view of America within pop culture is reflecting poorly on the country and that the answer is not censorship, but self-correction. She suggests that America once again invest in the export of American culture that reflects its artistic and literary heritage. Bayles is a critic of arts, music, media, and cultural policy, and author of Hole in Our Soul: The Loss of Beauty and Meaning in American Popular Music.

As you read, consider the following questions:

1. Bayles reports that foreign sales of US motion-picture and video products were valued at how much in 2005?

Martha Bayles, "The Return of Cultural Diplomacy," *Newsweek*, December 31, 2008.

2. What film and television show does the author give as examples of American exports that can damage America's reputation?

3. According to the author, where did the United States rank out of 50 countries in a 2008 ranking of culture?

Hollywood screenwriters get paid to come up with clever lines, so it's not surprising that when their organization, the Writers Guild West, held a panel discussion on American culture 15 months after 9/11 [2001, terrorist attacks], it gave it a catchy title: "We Hate You But Keep Sending Us 'Baywatch': The Impact of American Entertainment on the World." After a brief discussion, the panel concluded that apart from stereotyped portrayals of Muslims as terrorists, Hollywood was not to blame for America's plummeting global reputation.

The Exporting of American Pop Culture

One panelist, radio entrepreneur Norman Pattiz, cited global opinion surveys conducted in 2002 that showed disapproval of U.S. policies but approval of U.S. popular culture. Encouraged by such findings, Pattiz, a member of the Broadcasting Board of Governors (which oversees all U.S.-funded broadcasting), created Radio Sawa, an Arabic-language channel aimed at Arab youth that combines Western and Arabic pop music with U.S.-style news bulletins. The channel has become popular, but at the price of supplanting the more serious Voice of America Arabic service.

Radio Sawa is hardly the first government-funded use of popular culture to burnish America's image. During the cold war, Voice of America radio beamed jazz into the Soviet bloc. For more than a century, Washington has toiled to open foreign markets to Hollywood films and other forms of entertainment, on the assumption, articulated by President Woodrow Wilson, that popular culture "speaks a universal language [that] lends itself importantly to the presentation of America's plans and purposes." In other words, Americans have long believed that exporting movies, pop music, TV shows and other entertainment is both good business and good diplomacy. Is this belief still justified?

Regarding business, the answer is yes. The Bureau of Economic Analysis reports that between 1986 and 2005, foreign sales of U.S. motion-picture and video products rose from $1.91 billion to $10.4 billion (in 2005 dollars)—an increase of 444 percent. As Dan Glickman, president of the Motion Picture Association says, "Among all the sectors of the U.S. economy, our industry is the only one that generates a positive balance of trade in every country in which it does business." The same is true for the TV and music industries, and the reach is far greater when piracy is figured in.

Negative Views of US Cultural Exports

Diplomatically speaking, however, the picture is mixed. To be sure, police dramas like "Law & Order" and "CSI: Crime Scene Investigation" can expose those who live under authoritarian regimes to the rights and protections guaranteed by democracy. But when people with no other source of information about America take vulgar, violent, vitriolic examples of popular culture—the film "The Dark Knight," say, or the TV show "Desperate Housewives"—as an accurate reflection of reality, the impact can be negative and far-reaching. "People who watch U.S. television shows, attend Hollywood movies and listen to pop music can't help but believe that we are a nation in which we have sex with strangers regularly, where we wander the streets well armed and prepared to shoot our neighbors at any provocation, and where the lifestyle to which we aspire is one of rich, cocaine-snorting, decadent sybarites," writes Jerrold Keilson, the author of a State Department study of international visitors. Indeed, a 2007 report from the 47-nation Pew Global Attitudes Survey found consistently that "individuals who have traveled to the U.S. have more favorable views of the country than those who have not."

The same Pew survey also found that popular culture may no longer be America's best ambassador. "Majorities in several predominantly Muslim countries, including Bangladesh, Pakistan, Turkey, Jordan and Egypt, say they dislike American music, movies and television," the report said. "Indians and Russians also express negative views of U.S. cultural exports." Pew also uncovered a startling rise in the number of respondents agreeing with the statement "It's bad that American ideas and customs are spreading here." Since 2002, the percentage expressing disapproval grew by 17 points in Britain, 14 points in Germany and 13 points in Canada.

The Need to Self-Correct

President-elect [Barack] Obama's sheer charisma has already refreshed America's image. But it will take more than a new occupant in the White House to turn the entertainment industry around. Interestingly, Obama was the only candidate who confronted Hollywood directly, telling an audience of show-business luminaries in Los Angeles, "It is important for those in the industry to show some thought about who they are marketing [to] . . . I'm concerned about sex, but I'm also concerned about some of the violent, slasher, horror films that come out; you see a trailer, and I'm thinking, 'I don't want my 6-year-old or 9-year-old seeing that trailer while she's watching "American Idol"'."

Yet the solution is not to restrict popular entertainment exports. For one thing, America is faced with the worst economic crisis since the Great Depression, and every bit of revenue helps. Besides, plenty of countries regulate their own entertainment industries. When I asked a young actor in Mumbai whether gruesome American films such as the "Saw" series had many fans in India, he replied, "Of course not. They'd never get past the board." India's Central Board of Film Certification must approve all films released in that country. When I asked him whether India would be better off without censorship, the young actor's answer surprised me: "No. Filtering is needed."

Americans reject both government censorship and, in recent years, self-regulation by the entertainment industry. In any case, such limits are ineffectual; any attempt to censor would be quickly subverted by mass piracy and the Internet. But beyond these practical reasons, there is an important principle at stake. To censor American exports would be politically imprudent in a world of rising authoritarian powers (China, Russia, the Gulf states) that proudly dispense with American-style free speech. To defend their freedoms, Americans need to show that they are self-correcting—that the country possesses not only liberty but also a civilization worthy of liberty.

America's Heritage

Civilization? What civilization? I can already hear readers scoffing. America's rich artistic and literary heritage is increasingly unknown to the rest of the world—even to its friends. In Poland, I met a professor of American literature who confided in me that when she tells other Poles what she does for a living, they laugh and say, "That's impossible, there's no such thing!"

This anecdote is borne out by Simon Anholt, a member of the British Foreign Office Public Diplomacy Board who researches the global reputation of nations and cities. Together with the opinion research firm GfK Roper, Anholt conducts an annual survey of 1,000 online respondents in 20 countries who are asked to rank 50 nations according to such criteria as "governance," "people" and "investments." The Anholt-GfK Roper Nation Brands Index for 2008 ranks the United States 33rd for "culture." Notably, a previous survey that separated "popular culture" from "culture and heritage" ranked America dead last in the latter category. "The old idea that the U.S. is only good for popular culture and commerce has now hardened into a very negative perception," says Anholt.

The Need to Invest in American Culture

During the cold war, Washington strove to share America's cultural heritage through scholarly and professional exchanges, artist and writer tours, libraries, translations and culturally oriented international broadcasting. Any new investment in American "smart power" should include a substantial cultural component. But it won't be easy: ever since Sen. Jesse Helms attacked the National Endowment for the Arts in the 1980s for supporting works such as Robert Mapplethorpe's sadomasochistic photographs, American artists have expressed hostility toward their government, often through their art. Can the government be blamed for not wanting to export such work?

Still, plenty of artists do not trade in politicized shock. The way to reconcile democracy and civilization is to exercise good taste in ways that are open and communicable to all. One example: a 2004 production of Thornton Wilder's "Our Town" mounted by the U.S. Embassy in Cairo, performed in colloquial Arabic by some of Egypt's leading actors—a highly regarded and universally accessible bicultural treatment of home, community and the swift passage of time that showed just as the Abu Ghraib prison-abuse scandal was breaking.

In the same vein, U.S. radio broadcasters could take a cue from Radio Sawa. If pop music succeeds using the "together" approach, why not other forms of music? Why not fund a series of regional channels devoted to making Western and non-Western classics comprehensible to all listeners?

It is an American knack to present high culture not in a stuffy academic way but in a way that is both respectful and down to earth. To quote a favorite saying of [American songwriter] Cole Porter's, "Democracy is not a leveling down, but a leveling up." The American cultural ideal has always been to recognize art on its merits, regardless of where the artist hails from, and to make the finest fruits of civilization available to all. This ideal has never been fully realized. But that is no reason to abandon it, especially now when the country's ideals in general are in need of refurbishing.

Periodical and Internet Sources Bibliography

The following articles have been selected to supplement the diverse views presented in this chapter.

Martha Bayles	"Risky Business for Hollywood," *New York Times*, May 8, 2008.
David Brooks	"Ben Franklin's Nation," *New York Times*, December 14, 2010.
Danny Duncan Collum	"Our Fast-Food Empire," *Sojourners*, May 2006.
Tyler Cowen	"Some Countries Remain Resistant to American Cultural Exports," *New York Times*, February 22, 2007.
Simon Heffer	"America Is the Acceptable Face of Cultural Imperialism," *Telegraph* (UK), July 24, 2010.
Boris Kachka	"What the World Thinks About Us," *Conde Nast Traveler*, November 2008. www.concierge.com.
Richard Pells	"India, Europe, America: A Geocultural Triangle," *Chronicle of Higher Education*, December 8, 2006. http://chronicle.com.
Richard Pells	"The Decline and Fall of America's Cultural Dominance," *Dallas Morning News*, April 5, 2009.
Barnett Singer	"American 'Culture'—and Its Influence," *Contemporary Review*, Autumn 2008.
Mario Suttora	"The Italian Love Affair," *Newsweek International*, November 26, 2007.
Ethan Watters	"The Americanization of Mental Illness," *New York Times Magazine*, January 8, 2010.

For Further Discussion

Chapter 1

1. John Shattuck argues that the policies of the George W. Bush administration caused a decline in America's global reputation, whereas the Pew Research Center claims that Barack Obama's administration improved it. What are some of Shattuck's worries about reputation that the Pew Research Center notes as still being problematic under President Obama?

2. Richard Lowry and Ramesh Ponnuru give several examples of ways in which they believe American society is exceptional. What specific example does Damon Linker dispute? After considering both viewpoints, do you think this specific example given by Lowry and Ponnuru supports American exceptionalism? Why or why not?

Chapter 2

1. Robert Kagan argues that there are many situations worldwide that may call for US military intervention in the future. How might Harvey M. Sapolsky, Benjamin H. Friedman, Eugene Gholz, and Daryl G. Press argue that this is not an argument for the status quo on US military power?

2. Using specific textual passages, explain how Peter Brookes and Doug Bandow use the issue of America's reputation to reach contradictory conclusions.

3. John M. Owen IV, and Andrew C. McCarthy have different viewpoints on the efficacy of US democracy promotion in the world. Name at least one point of agreement between the two on the issue of democracy promotion in the Islamic world.

Chapter 3

1. Joy Gordon contends that economic sanctions that negatively impact the general population in Iran should be avoided. How might James Phillips respond that such negative impacts on the general population could lead to a good outcome?

2. Ian Vasquez expresses concern that foreign aid keeps governments from implementing solutions to its economic problems. Using this line of reasoning, how might Vasquez object to Laurie A. Garrett's claim that foreign assistance for global health programs should not be decreased?

Chapter 4

1. The viewpoints of the *The Economist*, Mortimer B. Zuckerman, and Martha Bayles all contend that the export of American culture is harming the reputation of the United States. Regarding the issue of reputation, name at least one point of agreement between two of these authors and one point of disagreement between two of these authors.

2. Do Richard Pells and Luis Martinez-Fernandez agree or disagree about the global impact of American culture? Use examples from the text to explain your answer.

Organizations to Contact

The editors have compiled the following list of organizations concerned with the issues debated in this book. The descriptions are derived from materials provided by the organizations. All have publications or information available for interested readers. The list was compiled on the date of publication of the present volume; names, addresses, phone and fax numbers, and e-mail and Internet addresses may change. Be aware that many organizations take several weeks or longer to respond to inquiries, so allow as much time as possible.

American Enterprise Institute for Public Policy Research (AEI)
1150 17th St. NW, Washington, DC   20036
(202) 862-5800 • fax: (202) 862-7177
e-mail: info@aei.org
website: www.aei.org

The American Enterprise Institute for Public Policy Research is a private, nonpartisan, nonprofit institution dedicated to research and education on issues of government, politics, economics, and social welfare. AEI sponsors research and publishes materials based on the principles of American freedom and democratic capitalism, through projects such as its Center for Defense Studies. AEI publishes *The American*, a bimonthly magazine, and a series of papers in its Economic Outlook series.

American Foreign Policy Council (AFPC)
509 C St. NE, Washington, DC   20002
(202) 543-1006 • fax: (202) 543-1007
e-mail: afpc@afpc.org
website: www.afpc.org

The American Foreign Policy Council is a nonprofit organization dedicated to bringing information to those who make or influence the foreign policy of the United States. AFPC provides resources to members of Congress, the executive branch, and the policy making community. AFPC publishes policy papers and numerous in-house bulletins, including *China Reform Monitor*, *Eurasia Security Watch*, and *Iran Democracy Monitor*.

Brookings Institution

1775 Massachusetts Ave. NW, Washington, DC   20036
(202) 797-6000
e-mail: communications@brookings.edu
website: www.brookings.edu

The Brookings Institution is a nonprofit public policy organization that conducts independent research. The Brookings Institution uses its research to provide recommendations that advance the goals of strengthening American democracy, fostering social welfare and security, and securing a cooperative international system. The Brookings Institution publishes a variety of books, reports, and several journals, including the book *Toughing It Out in Afghanistan*.

Cato Institute

1000 Massachusetts Ave. NW, Washington, DC   20001-5403
(202) 842-0200 • fax: (202) 842-3490
website: www.cato.org

The Cato Institute is a public policy research foundation dedicated to limiting the role of government, protecting individual liberties, and promoting free markets. The Cato Institute works to originate, advocate, promote, and disseminate applicable policy proposals that create free, open, and civil societies in the United States and throughout the world. Among the Cato Institute's many publications is the white paper, "Escaping the 'Graveyard of Empires': A Strategy to Exit Afghanistan."

Center for Defense Information (CDI)

1779 Massachusetts Ave. NW, Washington, DC   20036-2109
(202) 332-0600 • fax: (202) 462-4559

e-mail: info@cdi.org

website: www.cdi.org

The Center for Defense Information is an organization that works to promote discussion and debate on security issues such as nuclear weapons, space security, missile defense, and military transformation. CDI provides expert analysis on various components of national security, international security, and defense policy. CDI publishes reports, newsletters, *The Defense Monitor*, and books such as *Military Almanac 2007*.

Center for Security Policy

1901 Pennsylvania Ave. NW, Suite 201

Washington, DC   20006

(202) 835-9077 • fax: (202) 835-9066

e-mail: info@centerforsecuritypolicy.org

website: www.centerforsecuritypolicy.org

The Center for Security Policy is a nonprofit, nonpartisan national security organization that works to establish successful national security policies through the use of diplomatic, informational, military, and economic strength. Through its research, the Center for Security Policy aims to identify policies, actions, and resource needs that are vital to American security. The organization publishes the weekly *Policy Decision Briefs*, the weekly *The Americas Report*, and occasional papers, all of which are available at its website.

Center for Strategic and International Studies (CSIS)

1800 K St. NW, Washington, DC   20006

(202) 887-0200 • fax: (202) 775-3199

website: www.csis.org

The Center for Strategic and International Studies is a nonprofit organization that provides strategic insights and bipartisan policy solutions to decisionmakers. CSIS conducts research and analysis for policymakers in government, international institutions, the private sector, and civil society.

Among its many publications are the reports, "A Key to Success in Afghanistan: A Modern Silk Road Strategy" and "Iraq and the United States," both of which are available at its website.

Foreign Policy Research Institute (FPRI)
1528 Walnut St., Suite 610, Philadelphia, PA   19102
(215) 732-3774 • fax: (215) 732-4401
e-mail: fpri@fpri.org
website: www.fpri.org

The Foreign Policy Research Institute is an independent, nonprofit organization devoted to bringing the insights of scholarship to bear on the development of policies that advance national interests. FPRI conducts research on pressing issues and provides public education on international affairs. The organization publishes the quarterly *Orbis*, several periodical bulletins, and numerous essays, all of which are available at its website.

Institute for Cultural Diplomacy (ICD)
Keithstr. 14, Berlin   D-10787
   Germany
(011 49 30) 2360 768 0 • fax: (011 49 30) 2360 768 11
e-mail: info@culturaldiplomacy.org
website: www.culturaldiplomacy.org

The Institute for Cultural Diplomacy is an international, nongovernmental organization established to promote global peace and stability through strengthening and supporting intercultural relations. ICD's programs facilitate interaction among individuals of all cultural, academic, and professional backgrounds, from across the world. ICD performs research, some of which is available at its website, such as the article, "A New President, a New Era for CD? Will the US Move to a More Long-Term, Sustainable Policy on Cultural Diplomacy?"

Institute for Foreign Policy Analysis (IFPA)
1725 DeSales St. NW, Suite 402, Washington, DC   20036-4406

(202) 463-7942 • fax: (202) 785-2785
e-mail: dcmail@ifpa.org
website: www.ifpa.org

The Institute for Foreign Policy Analysis is an independent, nonpartisan research organization specializing in national security, foreign policy, and defense planning issues. IFPA helps senior government policymakers, industry leaders, and officials in the public policy community make decisions about global security. IFPA publishes numerous reports, including "Finding the Right Mix: Disaster Diplomacy, National Security, and International Cooperation."

Institute for Policy Studies (IPS)
1112 16th St. NW, Suite 600, Washington, DC   20036
(202) 234-9382
e-mail: info@ips-dc.org
website: www.ips-dc.org

The Institute for Policy Studies is a think thank that acts as a policy and research resource for progressive movements such as the anti-war movement. A project of the IPS, Foreign Policy in Focus, connects research and action of scholars, advocates, and activists seeking to make the United States a more responsible global partner. IPS publishes numerous reports available at its website, such as "Military vs. Climate Security: Mapping the Shift from the Bush Years to the Obama Era" and "The Cost of the Global Military Presence."

Norman Lear Center
Annenberg School for Communication and Journalism
at the University of Southern California
Los Angeles, CA   90089-0281
(213) 821-1343 • fax: (213) 821-1580
e-mail: enter@usc.edu
website: www.learcenter.org

The Norman Lear Center is a nonpartisan research and public policy center that studies the social, political, economic, and cultural impact of entertainment on the world. The Norman

Lear Center translates its findings into action through testimony, journalism, strategic research, and public outreach campaigns. The Norman Lear Center produces various publications, among which is the report, "Entertainment Goes Global: Mass Culture in a Transforming World."

US Department of Defense

1400 Defense Pentagon, Washington, DC   20301-1400
(703) 571-3343
website: www.defense.gov

The US Department of Defense is the federal department that supervises all agencies of the government related to national security and the armed forces. Among those agencies are the departments of Army, Navy, and Air Force; and the National Security Agency. The website of the Department of Defense contains news releases, photo essays, and reports, including "Measuring Stability and Security in Iraq—March 2010."

Bibliography of Books

Andrew J.   *The Limits of Power: The End of*
Bacevich   *American Exceptionalism.* New York:
                     Metropolitan Books, 2009.

John Bolton   *Surrender Is Not an Option:*
                     Defending America at the United
                     Nations and Abroad. New York:
                     Threshold Editions, 2008.

Amy Chua   *Day of Empire: How Hyperpowers*
                     Rise to Global Dominance—and Why
                     They Fall. New York: Doubleday,
                     2007.

Lane Crothers   *Globalization and American Popular*
                     Culture. Lanham, MD: Rowman &
                     Littlefield, 2006.

Thomas Donnelly *Lessons for a Long War: How America*
and Frederick   *Can Win on New Battlefields.*
Kagan, eds.   Washington, DC: AEI Press, 2010.

Tom Engelhardt   *The American Way of War: How the*
                     Empire Brought Itself to Ruin.
                     Chicago, IL: Haymarket Books, 2010.

Francis Fukuyama *America at the Crossroads.* New
                     Haven, CT: Yale University Press,
                     2006.

Leslie H. Gelb   *Power Rules: How Common Sense*
                     Can Rescue American Foreign Policy.
                     New York: Harper, 2009.

Mark L. Gillem   *American Town: Building the Outposts of Empire.* Minneapolis, MN: University of Minnesota Press, 2007.

Godfrey Hodgson   *The Myth of American Exceptionalism.* New Haven, CT: Yale University Press, 2009.

Chalmers Johnson   *Dismantling the Empire: America's Last Best Hope.* New York: Metropolitan Books, 2010.

Robert Kagan   *The Return of History and the End of Dreams.* New York: Knopf, 2008.

Andrew Kohut and Bruce Stokes   *America Against the World: How We Are Different and Why We Are Disliked.* New York: Times Books, 2006.

Ian S. Lustick   *Our Own Strength Against Us: The War on Terror as a Self-Inflicted Disaster.* Oakland, CA: The Independent Institute, 2008.

Michael Mandelbaum   *The Case for Goliath: How America Acts as the World's Government in the Twenty-First Century.* New York: Public Affairs, 2005.

William H. Marling   *How "American" Is Globalization?* Baltimore, MD: Johns Hopkins University Press, 2006.

Jack F. Matlock Jr.   *Superpower Illusions: How Myths and False Ideologies Led America Astray—and How to Return to Reality.* New Haven, CT: Yale University Press, 2010.

Rajan Menon   *The End of Alliances.* New York:
Oxford University Press, 2007.

Richard Pells   *Modernist America: Art, Music,
Movies, and the Global Impact of
American Culture.* New Haven, CT:
Yale University Press, 2011.

Kenneth M.   *A Path Out of the Desert: A Grand
Pollack   Strategy for America in the Middle
East.* New York: Random House,
2009.

Christopher A.   *The Power Problem: How American
Preble   Military Dominance Makes Us Less
Safe, Less Prosperous, and Less Free.*
Ithaca, NY: Cornell University Press,
2009.

Peter H. Schuck   *Understanding America: The Anatomy
and James Q.   of an Exceptional Nation.* New York:
Wilson, eds.   Public Affairs, 2008.

Strobe Talbott   *Great Experiment: The Story of
Ancient Empires, Modern States, and
the Quest for a Global Nation.* New
York: Simon & Schuster, 2009.

Ethan Watters   *Crazy Like Us: The Globalization of
the American Psyche.* New York: Free
Press, 2010.

Fareed Zakaria   *The Post-American World.* New York:
W.W. Norton, 2008.

Index

A

Abu Ghraib prison-abuse scandal, 213

Account 150 spending, 173–174

Acheson, Dean, 73

Addams, Jane, 56

Afghan National Army (ANA), 118

Afghan National Police (ANP), 118

Afghanistan
al Qaeda in, 107–108
democracy and, 135–136
global partnership and, 66
Iraq vs., 136–137
military intervention in, 16, 85, 93
Taliban threat, 107–110, 117, 122, 137–138
terrorism and, 23–24
threats from, 29
troop removal from, 81, 87–88

Afghanistan, war in
America's reputation over, 111–112
government, 120
India and, 110
Iran and, 111
necessity of, 112–113
operations, 120–121
overview, 106, 116–118
Pakistan and, 108–110
public support for, 121–122
security forces, 118–120
U.S. interests and, 115–116

Afghanistan Rights Monitor, 117, 120

Africa
American culture and, 186
destabilization in, 29, 66
foreign aid to, 148, 165–167, 176–177
Obama, Barack and, 37, 95, 128
sanctions and, 160

Ahmadinejad, Mahmoud, 158

Al-Jazeera, (Arabic news outlet), 188

al Qaeda, 92, 107–108, 115, 135–137

Allen, Woody, 186

Altman, Robert, 186

American culture
commercial success downside, 205–206
decentralization of, 188–189
disdain of, 191–194
export of, 194–195
global interest in, 184
globalization impact on, 187–188
as heritage, 212–213
in history, 184–186
importance of, 186–187
influence of, 185
investing in, 213–214
lack of skills, 200–201
literacy concerns with, 201–202
message in, 204–205
misunderstandings of, 199–200
opinion of, 206–207, 210–211